Know-It-All

Whiskey

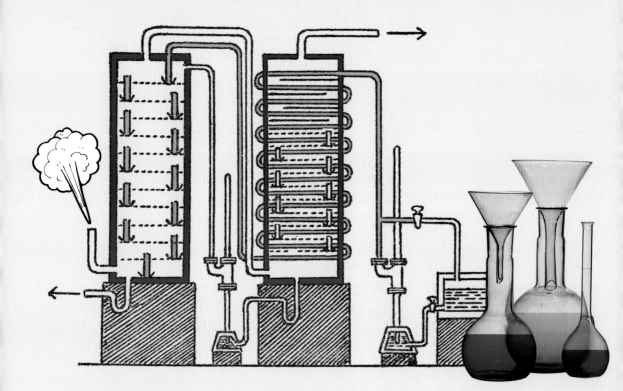

Know-It-All

Whiskey

The 50 Most Elemental Concepts of Whiskey, Each Explained in Under a Minute >

Editor **Charles MacLean**
Foreword **Ian Buxton**

Contributors

Davin de Kergommeaux
Alwynne Gwilt
Charles MacLean
Marcin Miller
Arthur Motley
Martine Nouet
Fionnán O'Connor
Hans Offringa
Andy Simpson
Gavin D. Smith

WELLFLEET
P R E S S

Inspiring | Educating | Creating | Entertaining

© 2017 Quarto Publishing plc

First published in 2017 by Wellfleet Press,
an imprint of The Quarto Group,
142 West 36th Street, 4th Floor,
New York, New York 10018, USA
T (212) 779-4972 F (212) 779-6058
www.QuartoKnows.com

Titles are also available at discount for retail, wholesale, promotional, and bulk purchase. For details, contact the Special Sales Manager by email at specialsales@quarto.com or by mail at The Quarto Group, Attn: Special Sales Manager, 401 Second Avenue North, Suite 310, Minneapolis, MN 55401, USA.

10 9 8 7 6 5 4 3 2 1

ISBN: 978-1-57715-162-3

This book was conceived, designed, and produced by
Ivy Press
An imprint of The Quarto Group
The Old Brewery, 6 Blundell Street
London N7 9BH, United Kingdom
T (0)20 7700 6700 F (0)20 7700 8066

Publisher Susan Kelly
Creative Director Michael Whitehead
Editorial Director Tom Kitch
Art Director Wayne Blades
Commissioning Editor Stephanie Evans
Project Editor Fleur Jones
Designer Ginny Zeal
Illustrator Nicky Ackland Snow
Picture Researcher Katie Greenwood

Printed in China

FSC
www.fsc.org
MIX
Paper from
responsible sources
FSC® C001701

CONTENTS

FOREWORD
Ian Buxton

I've been knocking around the drinks industry for near-on 30 years. I've been marketing director of a very well-known single malt; created a major industry conference; accidentally bought a (derelict) distillery; built several visitor centers; consulted on brands; written close to a dozen books; and generally engaged myself in the taxing business of drinking professionally. It's tough work, but someone has to do it.

So, I reckon to know a bit about whiskey and, believe me, there is a lot to learn. If you'd asked me I would have been skeptical about the idea of distilling (pun intended) all that knowledge into one little book. There's simply too much to cover, I would have said, and that's why there are literally hundreds of books on whiskey, some very, very detailed. No one could sensibly reduce all that to just 160 pages.

Well, I was wrong—though it did take a team of some of the very best writers to accomplish this, marshaled by the inimitable Charles MacLean whose own contributions are both insightful and lucid. *Know-It-All Whiskey* is a remarkable achievement and I'm happy to salute my colleagues' work. Not only is it a pleasure to look at, but it is also written with authority and real expertise, while remaining admirably concise. It is the perfect whiskey primer, though well-informed whiskey lovers will find much of interest. It can be dipped into or read from cover to cover and will be as useful as a quick reference guide as it is a source of new knowledge and a jumping-off point for further research. It is almost biblical in scope, but admirable in its brevity and in a world of instant comment, 140-character tweet wisdom, and punditry I cannot think of anything quite like it.

Know-It-All Whiskey is a thing of beauty and, in all probability, a joy forever. I strongly recommend pouring yourself a dram as you sit down to read. But make it a generous measure, as once you start reading you won't wish to stop. In the words of the immortal Robert Burns "Freedom and Whisky gang thegither!" Feel free to enjoy this refreshing draft of whiskey wit and wisdom, which I commend without reservation.

There are many different ways to enjoy your glass of whiskey. See page 140 for more about whiskey appreciation.

INTRODUCTION

Charles MacLean

These are exciting times for whiskey.

Indeed, never in its long and often dramatic history has there been so much activity. Never have so many new distilleries been opened and existing distilleries expanded in the so-called Big Five whisk(e)y-producing countries—Scotland, Ireland, the USA, Canada, and Japan. Never have there been so many distilleries springing up around the world—Taiwan and China, Australia and New Zealand, England and Wales, France and Germany, Belgium and the Netherlands, India, South America, Africa, Scandinavia, Italy, and Switzerland.

Consider the traditional producers. Since 2004, 21 distilleries have opened in Scotland, and I know of a further 44 that are proposed or under construction. The number of Irish distilleries has quadrupled, from three to 12. Operating Japanese distilleries have doubled, from six to 12, as have Canadian distilleries (from eight to over 40). And it is estimated that there are over 200 new plants in the USA, mostly small operations.

Such optimism is based upon the anticipated global demand for whiskey over the coming decades, which is currently estimated to grow at 4.2 percent year on year until at least 2020. But anticipating demand is a remarkably difficult exercise, vulnerable to factors beyond the industry's control, including the global economy and international politics, not to mention sale of alcohol regulations, fiscal arrangements, and fashion. Let us hope the marketers have got their sums right.

Interest in whiskey has grown steadily, then dramatically, since 1990. Various factors have contributed to this. First is the huge increase in choice, especially the availability of single malts—mainly Scottish, but also from Japan and new distilleries worldwide—and their high-end, non-Scotch variants—small batch bourbon and rye whiskeys, and more recently pure pot Irish whiskeys—each with its unique flavor profile. In 1970 only 30 single malts were available, and many of these were "uncommon." By 1980 this had doubled, and during the 1990s the stream became a torrent. Today it is impossible to measure the number of new releases in any one year—certainly in excess of 500.

Flavor wheels break down the aromas found in whiskey and provide a useful aid to appreciation. See also page 146.

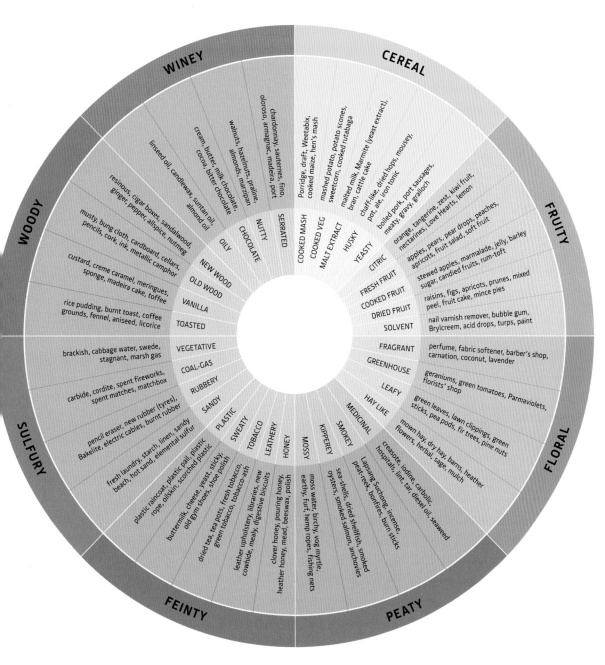

WHISKY MAGAZINE'S FLAVOR WHEEL

Increased choice led to increased availability. Retail chains began to dedicate shelf space to single malts, and by the early 1990s there was sufficient demand and range of stock to provide business for specialist retailers and for dedicated whiskey bars. Since selling prices for malts were appreciably higher than those for blends, greater profit margins could be made by retailers as well as brand owners; although single malts still account for less than 10 percent of the malt whiskey produced each year (the rest goes into blends), it contributes 25 percent by value.

Connoisseurship grew dramatically during the 1990s and continues to grow in every market. Not only is whiskey acknowledged to be the most complex spirit in the world, rewarding contemplation, it is also supremely versatile: It may be enjoyed in a wide variety of ways, at any time of the day or night.

Some would consider its flavor "challenging"—and it is an acquired taste—but once acquired, its devotees are passionately loyal. Whiskey clubs sprang up across Europe during the 1990s, soon followed by whiskey fairs and festivals—the Whisky Live organization now holds events in 20 countries each year, from Japan to Johannesburg, Taiwan to Toronto, Spain to South Africa—and there many more independent festivals.

Books about whiskey proliferated to satisfy consumers' thirst for information. Since 1980 five times as many books have been published on the subject as appeared in the previous 200 years. *Whisky Magazine* first appeared in 1998 and *Malt Advocate* (in America) in 1992; now there are numerous magazines dedicated to whiskey in America, France, Germany, the Netherlands, Switzerland, Japan, and China.

People began to collect malt whiskeys—the auctioneer Christie's held its first dedicated whiskey auction in London in 1989, and since the early 1990s McTear's in Glasgow have been holding four auctions a year; Bonhams in Edinburgh also hold quarterly whiskey auctions here and in Hong Kong and New York, while Sotheby's also hold regular whiskey sales in Hong Kong.

Prices achieved for some rare old whiskeys are eye-watering. A bottle of 1960 Karuizawa sold at auction in Hong Kong in 2015 for $118,548; at the same auction a set of 54 "Playing Cards" bottles from Hanyu Distillery went for $488,750. A bottle of 62-year-old Dalmore, which sold privately for $58,000 in 2005 (then a world record), was sold in Singapore in 2011 for $200,000. A single bottle of The Macallan achieved $628,000 at auction in Hong Kong in 2014. Since 2008, whiskey has consistently outperformed stock markets, and investors have joined consumers and collectors in pursuit of rare bottles.

My first task as editor of this book was to choose 50 topics that might serve as an introduction to the subject, then to invite ten colleagues—all experts in their fields—to write up each topic.

Designed to be supremely accessible, this book is divided into seven sections. Each opens with a glossary of terms and also includes a profile of a person who has played a significant role in the industry. Predictably, the first section, **Definitions**, explores the origins of whiskey and explains the different kinds of whiskey to be found around the world. The **History** section looks briefly at the historical foundations of the whiskeys made in the five leading whiskey-producing countries. **Production** follows, focusing on malt whiskey, but embracing grain whiskey production and blending, then the **Regional Differences** in the character of Scotch malt whisky are discussed, followed by the **National Differences** between the whiskeys made by the leading producing countries, and some of the more recent producers. **The Whiskey Trade** embraces a handful of disparate topics, including articles on buying, collecting, and investing, and the final section, **Appreciation** offers guidance on storing and serving, nosing and tasting, describing flavor, and pairing whiskeys with food.

Know-It-All Whiskey is a primer, not an encyclopedia. Hopefully it will stimulate interest in the world's most popular spirit drink and a desire to learn—and taste—more.

Slàinte!

DEFINITIONS

DEFINITIONS
GLOSSARY

ABV Percentage Alcohol by Volume (abbreviated to ABV) is the measure used throughout the world to express alcoholic strength, except in the USA, where American Proof also appears on the labels.

aqua vitae Latin for "water of life," which translates into Scots Gaelic as *uisge beatha* and into Irish Gaelic as *uisce beatha*.

alembic Derived from the Arabic *al'ambiq*. A distilling vessel with a gourd-shaped pot and a removable head equipped with a "beak" to condense the vapor.

beading test A crude method for ascertaining strength of alcohol whereby the liquid is vigorously shaken and the behavior of the resulting bubbles observed: If the liquid is under 50%ABV the bubbles last only a moment, above this they lie on the surface before dispersing.

blended grain whiskey A mix of grain whiskeys from different distilleries.

blended malt whiskey A mix of malt whiskeys from different distilleries.

blended whiskeys In the USA this is a mix of rye or bourbon whiskeys with neutral spirit, in proportions of no less than 20 percent of straight whiskey or a blend of straight whiskeys. Canadian whisky—the classic blended rye—blends whiskies made from single grain (corn, rye, wheat, barley) with fully matured lighter whiskies usually made from corn.

blended Scotch whisky A mix of malt and grain whiskies. Between five and 50 whiskies are typically used.

bourbon American whiskey made from a mash bill containing at least 51 percent corn (maize) spirit—typically around 80 percent—as well as smaller amounts of rye and wheat, known as "small grains." It must be distilled to a maximum of 80%ABV, matured in new, charred white oak barrels, and can be made anywhere in the USA.

continuous still A type of still that operates continuously, rather than in batches. Efficient and economical, the spirit produced is lighter than that produced in pot stills. Kentucky whiskey is distilled in a "hybrid continuous still." The "beer," or wash, is first distilled in a column still (the spirit being 55–0%ABV), then in either a "thumper" (a vessel containing water, through which the alcohol vapor passes, extracting any heavy elements) or in a "doubler"—a simple pot still.

hydrometer An instrument designed to measure the density of liquids.

pot still A still which operates in batches: It is charged with liquid, distilled off, cleaned, and charged again. Invariably the pot still is made from copper.

proof An old method of assessing the strength of alcohol by adding water and gunpowder. If the mixture ignites it is deemed to be "proved" or "at proof": If it fails to ignite it is "under proof" and should it ignite with a bang it is "over proof." Alcohol described as 100° UK (Imperial) proof is 57%ABV; 100° American proof is 50%ABV.

rye whiskey The original American whiskey, made and matured in a similar way to bourbon, except that the mash bill—the mix and proportions of grains used—must contain at least 51 percent rye, the "small grains" being wheat and malted barley. The term is commonly attached to Canadian whisky, which is correctly blended rye.

single grain whiskey The product of an individual distillery, made in continuous stills from mixed grains, predominantly wheat.

single malt whiskey The product of an individual distillery, made in pot stills from only malted barley.

specific gravity The relative density of a liquid, solid, or gas in relation to a standard—water in the case of liquids.

%Vol Alternative abbreviation for alcohol by volume (ABV).

WHAT IS WHISKEY?

The word "whiskey" derives from the Scots Gaelic *uisge beatha*, "water of life"—*aqua vitae* in Latin. The earliest written reference to distilled spirits (*aqua vitae*) in Scotland dates from 1494, when King James IV orders that one Friar John Cor be given eight bolls of malt, "to make aqua vitae." Given the primitive alembics of the time, this would still generate a considerable amount of spirit, around 200 liters of pure alcohol. Why the king wanted the *aqua vitae* is not known; in all likelihood for "medicinal use." The Royal Commission on Whiskey 1908/09 (note the "e") supplied the first legal definition as "a spirit obtained from a mash of cereal grains ... Scotch whisky as so defined, distilled in Scotland, and Irish whiskey, as so defined, distilled in Ireland." Such a definition meant that any kind of cereal could be used, not just malted barley, and that whiskey could legitimately be made in any type of still. In 1916 the Immature Spirits Act required that spirits made in Scotland and Ireland must be matured for three years before it could be named "whiskey"; later amendments were summed up by the Scotch Whisky Act 1988 and subsequent orders, consolidated by the Scotch Whisky Regulations 2009.

RELATED TOPICS
See also
SCOTCH & NON-SCOTCH
page 18

THE ALCHEMISTS
page 22

THE INVENTION OF WHISKEY
page 24

3-SECOND BIOGRAPHY
BILL WALKER
1942–
Teetotal Scottish MP who introduced the private member's bill which became the Scotch Whisky Act 1988

EXPERT
Charles MacLean

3-SECOND NIP
Broadly, the definition of Scotch whisky has been adopted by other countries, with some minor adjustments.

3-MINUTE DISTILLATION
Uisge beatha is pronounced "ooshkie-bayaha." The term was used colloquially from the early seventeenth century—"uisge" (c. 1618), "whiskie" (1715), "usky" (1736), "whisky (1746)—but officially the spirit was referred to as *aqua vitae* or *aquavite*. It has become customary for American and Irish distillers to name their product "whiskey," while for the rest of the world it is "whisky," but this is not a legal requirement.

No one knows for sure why King James IV ordered malt to be made into a large quantity of aqua vitae. He had a great interest in the scientific matters of the day, including alchemy.

SCOTCH & NON-SCOTCH

3-SECOND NIP
The vast majority of world whiskey is blended; only whisky made in Scotland can be called Scotch, and only around 8 percent of Scotch malt made is bottled as a single.

3-MINUTE DISTILLATION
The number of distilleries in Scotland has increased dramatically in recent years: Since 2004, 23 have opened and a further 42 are currently proposed. The same is true elsewhere: Ireland has grown from three to 12 distilleries in this period, the USA has added an astonishing 200 new distilleries. Every country in Europe now makes whiskey.

There are five styles of Scotch

whisky: single malt (a whisky from an individual distillery, made from malted barley in pot stills), single grain (also from one distillery, made from unmalted wheat or maize with a little barley malt), blended malt, blended grain, and blended Scotch. Japanese whisky makes the same distinctions. Traditional Irish whiskey is "pure pot still" (or "single pot still")—a mash of malted and unmalted barley, distilled in pot stills. Until recently it was difficult to find, having been overtaken by blended Irish whiskey (a mix of pure pot still with grain whiskey—rye, wheat, and (occasionally) oats, distilled in a continuous still). Ireland also makes pot-still malt and continuous-still grain whiskey. Most American whiskey is made in hybrid continuous stills. To be named "bourbon" or "rye" it must contain at least 51 percent of this grain, and must be matured in brand-new American oak. Tennessee whiskey, made the same way, is filtered through a bed of maple charcoal. Blended rye or bourbon is a mix of these whiskeys with up to 49 percent neutral spirit; blended American whiskey may have up to 80 percent neutral spirit. Although invariably called "rye," Canadian whisky is made by blending several whiskies each made exclusively from corn, rye, wheat, or barley.

RELATED TOPICS
See also
IRELAND
page 96

BOURBON
page 98

TENNESSEE WHISKEY
page 100

CANADA
page 102

JAPAN
page 104

3-SECOND BIOGRAPHY
GEORGE WASHINGTON
1732–99
A leading distiller himself, America's first President crushed the Whiskey Rebellion of 1794, which threatened the stability of the nascent United States

EXPERT
Charles MacLean

The United States, Canada, Ireland, Scotland, and Japan are the five countries that produce the most whisk(e)y.

SPIRIT STRENGTH

3-SECOND NIP
Proof is a measure of
the amount of ethanol
contained in an alcoholic
drink, which, in the United
States is calculated by
weight; elsewhere it is
reported by volume (ABV).

3-MINUTE DISTILLATION
In the eighteenth century,
distillers' license fees were
based on the estimated
amount of spirit their stills
could produce in a day.
They quickly came up
with still designs which
operated much more
rapidly. Only with accurate
hydrometers could tax be
based upon the amount
of ethyl alcohol in a given
quantity of spirits.

People have long been concerned about establishing the purity of metals and other materials by conducting tests, "proofs," or "assays." For spirits, various crude methods were used, such as the "beading test" where the liquid is vigorously shaken and the behavior of the resulting bubbles observed. The "gunpowder test" was the most commont: Mixed with gunpowder and water, the spirit was deemed to be "at proof" if the mixture ignited; if it did not, it was deemed "under proof." In 1675 Robert Boyle invented his New Essay Instrument or common hydrometer. It was capable of measuring the specific gravities (relative densities) of liquids, including a mix of alcohol and water. Boyle's hydrometer was improved by John Clarke in 1730 and adopted by the Board of Excise in 1787, but it was not reliably accurate and distillers could corrupt the readings by adding liquids like molasses. Bartholomew Sikes developed a greatly improved version in 1802, adopted 1817, which remained the standard until 1980, by which time electronic instruments had been developed to measure liquid densities. That year Proof was replaced throughout the European Union, including the UK, by "percentage of alcohol by volume" (%ABV, abbreviated to %Vol). Proof remains the measure for spirit strength in the USA, where 100° Proof = 50%ABV.

RELATED TOPIC
See also
WHAT IS WHISKEY?
page 16

3-SECOND BIOGRAPHIES
ROBERT BOYLE
1627–91
Anglo-Irish scientist who
coined the term "hydrometer"

JOHN CLARKE
d. 1789?
Scottish instrument-maker who
invented the first hydrometer
designed to measure the
density of liquids

BARTHOLOMEW SIKES
d. 1803
Secretary to the Excise Board
1774–83; he won a competition
to find a better hydrometer
than Clarke's, but died before
he could claim £2,000 for the
rights, which went to his widow

EXPERT
Charles MacLean

Invented by Robert Boyle in 1675, the hydrometer measured the relative densities of water and alcohol in whiskey as well as other liquids.

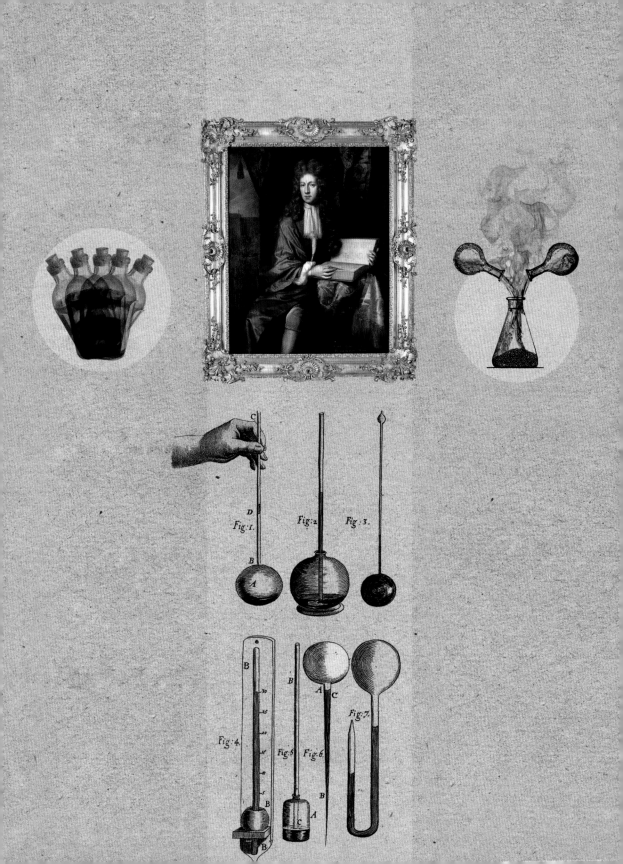

Early 300s
First-known books on
alchemy produced, the
work of Egyptian mystic
Zosimos of Panopolis

850
Corpus of works by Jābir
ibn Hayyān (Geber)
translated into Latin as
De Summa Perfectionis

936–1013
Life of Abulcasis, Spanish
Muslim physician and
early distiller

c. 1220–92
Life of Roger Bacon or
"Doctor Mirabilis," English
Franciscan and alchemist

455
Rome falls to the Vandals,
Imperial authority
collapses in the West

850
Al Kindi's *Kitab al-Asrar*
(*Book of Secrets*)
provides an early account
of an alembic

c. 1175–1232
Life of Michael Scot—
Scottish expatriate,
alchemist, Arabic
translator, and teacher
at Salerno, Europe's
first medical school

c. 1290
Arnoldus de Villa Nova,
a Catholic Spanish
chemist and Arabic
translator, writes the
first European manual
of distilling

711
Moorish Invasion of the
Iberian Peninsula

854–925
Life of Rhazes, Persian
alchemist and chief
physician practicing at
the Baghdad Hospital
at the heart of the
Caliphate, author of
Sirr al'Asrar (*Secret
of Secrets*)

1225
Michael Scot writes his
Lumen Luminum, making
the first references by a
Christian European to the
science of distillation

Early 1300s
The *Red Book of Ossory*,
written at Kilkenny
Cathedral, provides the
first Irish references to
distillation and to *aqua
vitae*, the water of life

c. 720–1258
The Islamic Golden Age.
The Caliphate plans to
translate all of human
understanding into the
Arabic language

THE ALCHEMISTS

Long before it was applied to liquor, the Latin verb *distillare* simply meant "to drip" and natural philosophers have been trying to drip out the essences of fluids since the days of Aristotle. Whether filtered through cloth or heated and cooled in kettles and condensers, these early *distillates* were regarded as philosophical purifications of the natural world by early thinkers of the late Hellenistic, Gnostic Christian, and Islamic philosophies that swept through Alexandrine Egypt as various cultures ebbed and converged. Although the alchemists are now remembered for their attempts to achieve immortality and to *purify* base metals into gold, many of these men were essentially early chemists. (The two words even share an etymology.) Even during their lifetimes, however, their smoke-stained experiments often seemed slightly more spiritual, and especially in a world in which science and theology were inextricably linked.

The oldest-known alchemical texts were written by the gnostic mystic Zosimos, who even compared distillation to baptism. Although Zosimos gives us our first descriptions of something like a still (an invention he ascribed to an even older alchemist, Maria the Jewess), the ineffective cooling and weak glass of the era didn't allow for the distillation of anything more volatile than water. So, no alcohol for him.

Egyptian mystics aside, distillation is really the brainchild of a generation of brilliant physicians who emerged during the Islamic Golden Age as the spreading Caliphate absorbed the ideas of Arabia, Persia, North Africa, Spain, and Egypt itself. In his *Secret of Secrets*, the Persian alchemist Rhazes outlined the basic components of a modern alembic, while his subtler heating mechanisms allowed for more refined distillations. As Moorish Spain thrust Europe into close contact with Islam, the works of alchemists like Rhazes, Avicenna, and their European admirers, Roger Bacon and Michael Scot, were widely read as the "Eastern Sciences" took hold across monasteries and universities.

From Rhazes to Roger, these alchemists were often simply regarded as wizards by their contemporaries but, with mist and mythos briefly evaporated, the fathers of distillation were deeply sceptical scientific inquirers. They may never have discovered the Philosopher's Stone, but the immortal testament to the innovativeness of their thinking may be that, even today, the pot still's inventors are still regarded through the same hazy eyes so often inspired by the distillates it drips.

Fionnán O'Connor

THE INVENTION OF WHISKEY

The roots of whiskey's evolution

lie in the birth of distilled spirits. Distillation describes the separation of a liquid by evaporation and condensation. Based on earlier models by the Coptic Egyptians, the still or alembic was born from the eighth- and ninth-century efforts of Islamic alchemists to obtain medical essences and perfumes from base ingredients: Alchemy, alembic, and alcohol are all Arabic words. The alembic works by heating a liquid until it evaporates to separate out substances with different volatilities, then trapping the purified forms as they condense during cooling. This device evolved into the pot still, without which there would be no whiskey. The Moorish occupation of Sicily and the Iberian peninsula brought Europe into close contact with the Arabic sciences and use of the alembic soon traveled across monasteries and medical schools, where it was eventually applied to wine, leading to a series of brandy-like elixirs referred to as *aqua vitae* or the water of life. As the spirit spread, the new liquor quickly adapted to both local ingredients and local languages. Having very little wine, the Gaels of Northern Europe started using ale and thus the earliest whiskeys were born.

3-SECOND NIP
The Scots, the Irish, the Arabs, and the monks—depending on who you ask, all invented whiskey... but whiskey wasn't invented: It evolved.

3-MINUTE DISTILLATION
Before the Middle Ages, Europeans drank their alcohol fermented—beer, mead, wine but no spirits. The hard stuff only arrived during the early medieval period via the Moorish invaders in Spain. Although the monks of Ireland and, later, Scotland may have given us our earliest whiskeys, the stuff they distilled tasted nothing like a modern malt. Clear, unaged, and usually mixed with herbs and honey, these monastic liquors were originally medicines and tonics, before being adopted as social drinks.

RELATED TOPIC
See also
POT STILL DISTILLATION
page 58

3-SECOND BIOGRAPHY
ARNOLDUS DE VILLA NOVA
c. 1240–1311
Catalan physician and pharmacist who wrote the first European manual of distilling and was said to remark that distilled wine or *aqua vitae* (water of life) could "lead to vigor and creative ecstasy"

EXPERT
Fionnán O'Connor

Distillation has its origins over 1,000 years ago, although the spirits first distilled by alchemists and monks were very different to those we are familar with today.

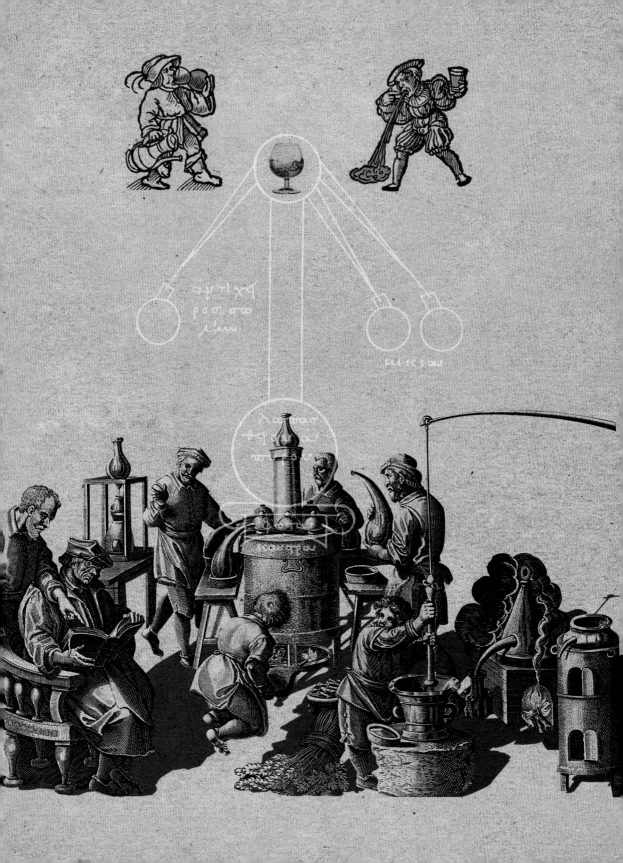

HISTORY

blended American whiskey This is permitted to contain a minimum of only 20 percent straight whiskey, the rest being neutral spirit. It is cheaper to make, lighter bodied, and blander to taste.

Coffey still Also named a "patent still" to describe the type of column still invented by Aeneas Coffey in 1830.

column still The American equivalent of the Coffey, patent, or continuous still. The name derives from the shape of the still, which usually has two tall copper columns, 40–50 feet (12–15 meters) in height. The first column, the analyzer, separates the spirit from the wash; the second, the rectifier, concentrates and purifies the spirit. Depending on the degree of purification required, there may be up to five columns.

draff The husks and spent grain residues left after mashing. A nutritious cattle food, draff is either taken from the distillery wet by local farmers or sent off to a "dark grains plant" to be mixed with pot ale, dried, and pelletized as cattle cake.

Excise Act An Act of Parliament relating to excise duties.

excise duty A tax on certain goods and commodities, including alcohol, produced and sold within a country.

moonshine Illegally distilled homemade whiskey, usually with a very high alcohol content. Known as "white dog" in the USA, "peatreek" in Scotland, and "poitín'" in Ireland.

Prohibition The prevention by law of the manufacture and sale of alcohol, especially in America between 1920 and 1933.

pure pot still Now marketed as "single pot still," this is the traditional whiskey of Ireland, and also the most flavorful, distilled from a mix of malted and unmalted barley and other grains. However, according to Irish law, any whiskey made in a pot still may claim the name. Until 2013, pure pot still was rare, then Irish Distillers thankfully introduced several more brands.

straight whiskey Literally whiskey to which water has not been added, but specifically applied to "straight bourbon" and "straight rye" in the USA, made according to the legal definition of such spirits.

wash This is fermented wort at around 8% Vol—not unlike a strong, unhopped ale.

wort A sweet, sticky semitransparent liquid that is essentially unfermented beer.

THE HISTORY OF SCOTCH

3-SECOND NIP
Although written evidence of malt distilling dates from 1494 and large commercial distilleries appeared in the 1770s, today's Scotch whisky industry dates from 1823.

3-MINUTE DISTILLATION
Scotch whisky has a history of peaks and troughs. The surge in licensed distilling after 1823 declined during the 1840s; the 1890s boom turned dramatically to bust in 1900; that of the post-war period foundered during the mid-1970s. Since 2005 the industry has experienced an unprecedented boom—23 new distilleries have opened since 2004; 42 new ones are currently proposed. But will it last?

The Excise Act of 1823 halved duty and made it possible for small distillers to make good whisky economically. Between 1823 and 1830, 232 distilleries were licensed, though many failed during the "Hungry 40s": by 1844, 169 plants operated. Significantly, a radically new design of still, perfected by Aeneas Coffey in the late 1820s, was capable of distilling continuously (unlike pot stills) and rapidly, and of producing very pure, high-strength spirits. Gradually Coffey stills were adopted by grain distillers. The resulting spirits, though, were bland compared with pot-still malts, and soon spirits merchants were mixing the two to create blended Scotch of consistent flavor and quality. The foundations of many great blending houses were laid in this period by men like Andrew Usher, John Dewar, Johnnie Walker, Matthew Gloag, Arthur Bell, George Ballantine, and William Teacher, and their sons responded vigorously to the demand for blended Scotch in the 1880s and 90s. By 1900, when there was a severe downturn, largely due to overproduction, the malt-distillers' key customers were the blenders and single malts were rare. By the time of the Second World War, blended Scotch was again fashionable and continued into the 1970s, before another downturn caused more distillers to release their products as single malts.

RELATED TOPICS
See also
SMUGGLING
page 32

THE BLENDING HOUSES
page 116

3-SECOND BIOGRAPHIES
AENEAS COFFEY
1780–1852
Former Inspector General of Excise in Dublin, who perfected a continuous still that was designed by Robert Stein, a scion of the leading Scottish distilling dynasty

ANDREW USHER I
1782–1855
Generally considered to be the "father of whisky blending" who released his first blend, Usher's Old Vatted Glenlivet, in 1853; he learned his skills from his wife

EXPERT
Charles MacLean

Aeneas Coffey's continuous column still revolutionized whisky production, and laid the foundations for the great blending houses.

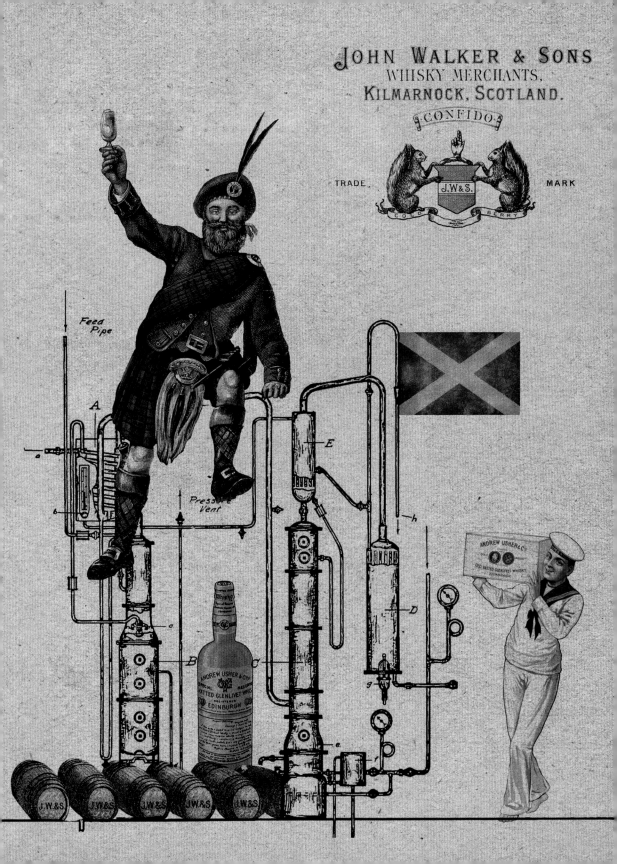

SMUGGLING

The first "Excyse Act" was passed

by the Scottish Parliament on January 31, 1644, and imposed duty on "everie pynt of aquavytie or strong watteris sold within the country." The tax applied equally to imported and homemade spirits, but *only* if the spirits were sold. Distilling for domestic consumption, from grains grown by a local community or landowner, was legal until 1781. When it was banned, "the country was convulsed by smuggling operations of all kinds…" Distilling, like brewing, was considered a natural right; landlords knew that tenants would be more able to pay rents if they sold whisky, and, as magistrates, they were lenient to offenders. The Highlands were impossible to police: In spite of the seizure of nearly 2,000 stills in 1782, it was estimated that 21,000 stills remained in operation, and when duty began to rise steeply after war was declared against France in 1793, smuggling became endemic. After 1815, the authorities and landed classes became increasingly afraid of republicanism and anarchy: If smugglers could flout the Excise laws, all laws might be flouted. Parliament was persuaded to amend the legislation to allow small distillers to make and sell good whisky at a reasonable profit. In return, landowners helped to suppress illicit distilling by evicting tenants convicted of smuggling. The result was the Excise Act 1823.

3-SECOND NIP
Strictly speaking, "smuggling" means "to import or export illegally, or to convey secretly," but, in Scotland, its meaning was extended to distilling whisky illegally.

3-MINUTE DISTILLATION
Distilling was an essential part of the farming year. Not only did it allow surplus cereal crops to be saved from rot and rodents and turned into cash, or bartered, the residues— draff and spent grains— were the only fodder available in the Highlands to sustain cattle during winter. And since the Highland economy was based on cattle, farmers had no option but to distill outside the law.

RELATED TOPIC
See also
THE HISTORY OF SCOTCH
page 30

3-SECOND BIOGRAPHY
ALEXANDER, 4TH DUKE
OF GORDON
1743–1827
The largest landowner in northern Scotland, who urged Parliament in 1820 to encourage small distillers to take out licenses; the resulting Act laid the foundations of the modern whisky industry

EXPERT
Charles MacLean

Alexander, 4th Duke of Gordon was influential in helping Highlanders to obtain licenses for their illicit distilleries.

IRISH WHISKEY

RELATED TOPIC
See also
PROHIBITION
page 40

EXPERT
Fionnán O'Connor

3-SECOND NIP
The birthplace of whiskey, steeped in centuries of illicit moonshine, Ireland has restored its reputation for producing some of the world's finest traditional malt, and pot-still whiskeys.

3-MINUTE DISTILLATION
Outselling Scotch three cases to one, Ireland's nineteenth-century pure pot-still distillers seemed invincible and were dismissive of rapidly produced grain whiskeys and blends. As blended whiskey boomed, American Prohibition and Ireland's war of independence boiled up a perfect storm for the Irish alternative's industrial collapse. The surviving distillers finally embraced the blend in the 1960s. Ironically, the success of these silky blends has led to a renaissance among the malt and Irish pot-still legends blending once made obsolete.

Although there are several early records of medicinal spirits, the first account of someone actually enjoying the drink comes from *The Annals of Clonmacnoise* (1405), the translation of an Irish chronicle, which recalls the death of Risteard MacGrannell from "a surfeit of aqua vitae, to that man aqua mortis." Not exactly a steady start, but by the time the British government started paying attention to private distilling in the 1500s, the water of life was a household sip. In those days, whiskey was made with malted remains from a farmer's crop and drunk straight from the still with maybe some herbs. This all came to a halt in the 1700s when homemade whiskey was banned, an excise was levied on professional distillers, and even malt became taxable. Many farmers ignored the law and made their own "little pot" or *poitín* (moonshine) whiskey illegally. It was the new caste of licensed distillers, however, who would ultimately shape not only the tale but the taste of the drink they distilled. Dodging taxes by mixing in unmalted *green* barley, they created a thick gingery style that became so popular that, even after the malt tax was repealed, their recipe remained.

Once producing among the most popular whiskeys in the world, the Irish whiskey industry was hit heavily by industrial collapse in the late nineteenth century. Recent decades have seen a resurgence in popularity.

AMERICAN WHISKEY

No one knows when whiskey

was first distilled in what is now the United States of America, but settlers from many nations, particularly from Europe, brought with them knowledge of the art of distillation. According to the Distilled Spirits Council of the United States (DISCUS), "In 1640, William Kieft, the Director General of the New Netherland Colony, decided that liquor should be distilled on Staten Island. His master distiller, Wilhelm Hendriksen, is said to have used corn and rye to make liquor, and since the Dutch didn't develop a formula for gin until ten or so years later, he must have been making some form of whiskey." Title 27 of the US Code of Federal Regulations enshrines the legal definition of "American whisky"—note the Scottish/Canadian spelling of "whisky" was used—as: "an alcoholic distillate from a fermented mash of grain produced at less than 190° proof in such manner that the distillate possesses the taste, aroma, and characteristics generally attributed to whisky, stored in oak containers (except that corn whisky need not be so stored), and bottled at not less than 80° proof." The Regulations then outline specific definitions for bourbon, rye, wheat, malt, corn, blended, and "straight whisky."

RELATED TOPICS
See also
SCOTCH & NON-SCOTCH
page 18

SPIRIT STRENGTH
page 20

BLENDING
page 66

BOURBON
page 98

EXPERT
Gavin D. Smith

American whiskeys and bourbons can be made from four different types of grain: rye, wheat, barley, and corn.

BOURBON CORDIAL.

780
Robert Samuels begins
to farm and distill in the
state of Kentucky

844
The Samuels family
commences commercial
distillation at Deatsville

910
Bill Samuels born in
Bardstown, Kentucky

936
Bill becomes distillery
manager of the rebuilt
Deatsville plant

938
Appointed president of
T. W. Samuels & Son

943
Leaves the business

953
Buys Burks' Distillery
at Loretto

1954
Production of whiskey
begins at Burks' Distillery

1958
First bottling of Maker's
Mark, featuring the
brand's red wax seal

1980
Burks' Distillery
designated a National
Historic Landmark

1981
Sale of company to
Hiram Walker & Sons,
retirement of Bill Samuels

October 1992
Bill Samuels dies in
Louisville, Kentucky

y

BILL SAMUELS

T. William "Bill" Samuels Sr. was a sixth-generation distiller, born in Bardstown, Kentucky. His family's origins in the state could be traced back to 1780, when one Robert Samuels moved from Pennsylvania to farm and distill there. The family began commercial whiskey-making at Deatsville in 1844, and ultimately Bill Samuels, who had trained as an engineer, became manager and then president of the distillery at Deatsville which his father, Leslie, had rebuilt after the end of Prohibition in 1933, along with external investors.

Bill Samuels dissociated himself from the business a decade later, but in October 1953 proceeded to purchase, for $35,000, a rundown distillery at Loretto, which had been founded by Charles Burks in 1805. Samuels set about restoring it, and renamed it The Star Distillery. The site was listed on the National Register of Historic Places in 1974, and designated a National Historic Landmark in December 1980 as "Burks' Distillery."

According to legend, before starting to distill, Bill Samuels proceeded to do something truly radical. He ceremoniously burnt the only copy of his grandfather Robert's bourbon recipe, setting fire to the curtains in the process! Samuels was convinced that the future of bourbon lay in creating a smooth, less harsh spirit, and he experimented by baking bread using varying combinations of barley, corn, and wheat. He settled on a recipe that used winter wheat rather than rye, thus influencing a gradual revolution across the entire bourbon industry. He did, however, maintain an element of continuity by using the same strain of yeast that had previously been used in the family's Deatsville distilleries.

Whiskey production began in 1954, and the first bottles, of what were branded Maker's Mark, hit the shelves four years later. The name came courtesy of Samuels' wife, Margie, who was a collector of pewter, and noted that each piece carried a hallmark, or "maker's mark," signifying that the producer was proud of his or her creation. It was also Margie's idea to hand-dip the bottle necks in red wax. In tribute to his Scottish heritage, Bill Samuels decided to use the spelling "whisky" on the labels. Sold in distinctive squarish bottles, it is still America's only small-batch bourbon that has never been mass-produced. It is aged for about six years and its rich flavor is said to derive from distillation to the lowest proof.

In 1981 Maker's Mark was sold to Hiram Walker & Sons of Canada, at which point Bill Samuels retired from active involvement in the company. However, his son Bill Samuels Jr. continued the family connection with Maker's Mark, becoming president and CEO in 1975. He retired in 2011, and was succeeded by his son Rob in the role of CEO.

Gavin D. Smith

PROHIBITION

The seed for Prohibition was

sown in 1874 by the Women's Christian Temperance Union (WCTU). Their president, Frances Willard, advocated a peaceful approach, singing psalms and preaching the dangers of demon alcohol. Mr. Wayne Wheeler of the Anti-Saloon League, who used considerable political influence to get Prohibition on the agenda, joined forces with the WCTU in 1893. In 1919 the US government was convinced and prepared a law banning alcoholic beverages. The *Volstead Act* passed on January 20, 1920, made it illegal to produce, distribute, and sell "intoxicating liquors." Exceptions were made for medicinal and religious purposes. Nicknamed "The Noble Experiment," Prohibition utterly failed and created an estimated annual $50,000,000 tax deficit. Smuggling spawned an unprecedented wave of crime, with gangsters like Al Capone cashing in on the proceeds. People made "bathtub gin" at home, often poisonous, causing blindness and paralysis. Financially, healthwise, and morally Prohibition resembled a road to perdition. Of course this could not continue. On December 5, 1933, President Franklin D. Roosevelt announced Repeal as part of regulations in his New Deal Program to recover the struggling economy. The Noble Experiment ended and the whiskey industry had to reinvent itself.

3-SECOND NIP
In 1920 the USA went dry for 13 years, destroying its distilling industry and causing a wave of organized crime; How could this have happened?

3-MINUTE DISTILLATION
Not all proponents of Prohibition were peaceful. Mrs. Carrie Nation wielded a hatchet in saloons, destroying bottles of whiskey behind the bar and crying "men are nicotine-soaked, beer-besmirched, whiskey-greased red-eyed devils." Her followers sold miniatures of her hatchet as souvenirs, to bail her out of jail. On the other side Al Capone washed his hands in innocence, defending himself with the remark: "All I ever did was supply a demand that was pretty popular."

RELATED TOPICS
See also
AMERICAN WHISKEY
page 36

CANADIAN WHISKY
page 42

3-SECOND BIOGRAPHIES
CARRIE NATION
1846–1911
American activist and temperance advocate

AL CAPONE
1899–1947
Infamous American gangster and boss of the crime-based empire the "Chicago Outfit"

EXPERT
Hans Offringa

The entire American nation went dry when the Volstead Act was passed in January 1920. The Women's Christian Temperance Union perceived alcohol as the root cause of numerous social problems.

DEPARTMENT OF JUSTICE BUREAU OF INVESTIGATION
IDENTIFICATION DIVISION, WASHINGTON, D.C.

CRIMINAL HISTORY

CANADIAN WHISKY

3-SECOND NIP
Two centuries in the making, Canadian whisky's origins lie in innovative waste management by flour millers who recycled leftovers into a distinct new whisky style.

3-MINUTE DISTILLATION
Canadian whisky operates under an American shadow. Disruption during the Civil War made the USA Canada's largest customer. Then, Prohibition created a lucrative gray market for some, but the loss of legal US sales left many Canadian distilleries on the brink of bankruptcy. Changing consumer tastes from whisky to white spirits in the 1980s resulted in distillery closures. Where once there were nearly two dozen, seven remained. Things turned around in 2013, with new confidence, flavor, sales, and distilleries.

For Canada, drinking was a rum deal at first. Irish and Scottish immigrants in the eighteenth and nineteenth centuries knew that making rum was easier than whisky. Consequently, that is what they distilled. Whisky waited on the nineteenth-century arrival of English and European millers in central Canada. Wheat-filled mills distilled their excesses in column stills, some made from wood, displacing the tiny copper pot stills settlers had brought from their homelands. German and Dutch immigrants, remembering rye schnapps, convinced local distillers to add rye flour to their all-wheat mashes. "Rye" became the name of the resulting flavorful whisky style. In 1887, Canada introduced the world's first whisky-aging law and commercial distilling quickly eclipsed small-time, quick-sale operators. Then, American politics gave rival Canadian entrepreneurs Sam Bronfman and Harry Hatch new opportunities. Throughout Prohibition they sold imported and Canadian whisky—legally and profitably—to agents of US crime rings. Bronfman built Seagram's global distilling empire, and Hatch acquired Corby, Wiser, Gooderham & Worts, and Hiram Walker distilleries in Canada. After decades of growth, the 1980s brought a period of relative obscurity. Today, as interest in whisky advances globally, Canadian whisky is a contender once more.

RELATED TOPICS
See also
PROHIBITION
page 40

CANADA
page 102

3-SECOND BIOGRAPHIES
HIRAM WALKER
1816–99
American distiller who commuted daily from the USA to Canada where he created Canadian Club

J.P. WISER
1825–1911
Animal breeder whose whisky remains a century-long bestseller, but his original distillery's prime product was cattle feed

EXPERT
Davin de Kergommeaux

American entrepreneur Hiram Walker founded his distillery in Ontario in 1858 and went on to create Canadian Club, one of Canada's top export whiskies.

JAPANESE WHISKY

3-SECOND NIP

Masataka Taketsuru and Shinjiro Torii are the fathers of the Japanese whisky industry; the companies they founded, Nikka and Suntory respectively, continue to dominate.

3-MINUTE DISTILLATION

Hanyu and Karuizawa distilleries were built during a period of economic growth and succumbed to the reverse; both closed in 2000. Ironically, their quality and, in particular, rarity now contributes to the stratospheric increase in auction prices being paid for Japanese single malts. A single, record-breaking bottle of Karuizawa 1960 Cask #5627 (one of 41) sold at Bonhams (Hong Kong) in August, 2015, for HK$918,750 (the equivalent at the time of $118,467).

Japan's relationship with whiskey can be traced back to 1854. When Commodore Matthew Perry arrived with gunships to "negotiate" the Treaty of Kanagawa, he brought the Emperor a precious gift—a quantity of American whiskey. In Japan, the production of Western-style spirits began at the tail end of the nineteenth century but with more emphasis on chemistry than on nosing or blending. Then, in July 1918, Masataka Taketsuru, a young chemist with an interest in distilling, ventured to Scotland to learn how to make whisky. On his return in 1921, he was employed by the visionary Shinjiro Torii; Japan's first recognizable whisky distillery was founded in 1924 at Yamazaki, near Kyoto, an area prized by sake-brewers for the quality of its water. In 1934 Taketsuru built his own distillery, Yoichi, on Hokkaido, Japan's northern island. The ending of the Second World War saw an increase in Japanese whisky production: Hanyu was constructed in 1946 (although single malt production only began there in 1980), and Karuizawa in 1955; growth surged through the late 1960s and early 1970s with Suntory, Nikka, and others opening new distilleries. The unprecedented success of Japan's whiskies at international competitions since 2001 has led to an unforeseen boom in popularity.

RELATED TOPICS

See also
MASATAKA TAKETSURU
page 106

INVESTING IN WHISKEY
page 132

3-SECOND BIOGRAPHIES
MATTHEW C. PERRY
1794–1858
US Navy Commodore and diplomat who sought to establish links between Japan and the Western world

SHINJIRO TORII
1879–1962
Japanese pharmaceutical wholesaler who founded a drinks business that became Suntory, the world's third largest spirits maker

EXPERT
Marcin Miller

Commodore Matthew Perry's gift of whiskey to the Japanese emperor in 1854 marked the beginning of Japan's passion for and success in the whisky industry.

PRODUCTION

analyzer The first column in a continuous still, which strips the alcohol from the wash In the USA, wash is known as "beer," and the analyzer as a "beer still."

enzymes A substance produced by a living organism which acts as a catalyst to bring about a specific biochemical reaction. The legal definition of "whisk(e)y" in most countries requires that the enzymes must come from within the cereal grains (endogenous). Canada allows the addition of enzymes (exogenous).

feints The late runnings of the spirit still. Pungent and impure, they are sent to a separate vessel to be re-distilled.

foreshots The early runnings of the spirit still. High strength, pungent, and impure, they are sent to a separate vessel to be re-distilled.

fraction The portions into which a mixture of alcohol and water may be separated by distillation.

green malt Barley which has been "modified" (i.e. converted into malt by steeping and germinating), but not dried.

grist Ground malt. It has three portions: grits, husk, and flour.

heart The pure middle portion of the spirit run, saved to be filled into cask. The early runnings are "foreshots," the later ones "feints."

lauter tun A modern stainless steel mash tun, invented by the brewing industry in Germany. There are two types: the semi-Lauter tun, with four revolving arms to which are attached vertical rakes, to stir the mash, and the full-Lauter tun, wherein the arms may be raised and lowered as well as revolve, making for an even gentler process.

low wines The liquid arising from the first distillation in the wash (or low wines) still, at around 21%ABV.

mash The mixture of grist and hot water.

mash tun The vessel in which the mixture of grist and hot water is "mashed." Enzymes within the grist convert the starch into various sugars, which dissolve in the hot water, becoming "wort."

mouthfeel The feeling and texture of liquid in the mouth. Typical descriptors for whiskey are: smooth, creamy, oily, hot, peppery, mouth-cooling, astringent, spritzich, etc.

pot ale The high protein residue of liquid from the wash still, once the alcohol has been driven off. Also known as "burnt ale" or "spent wash," it contains around 4 percent solids, which, following evaporation into a syrup (40–50 percent solids), is combined with draff to make cattle cake.

rectifier The second column in a continuous still, which purifies and raises the alcoholic strength of the spirit.

rickhouse These are the very tall maturation warehouses typically used in Kentucky, where summer and winter temperatures are extreme resulting in a more rapid maturation, especially toward the top of the rickhouse. On account of this, the whiskey matures at different rates, and American distillers move their barrels from one level to another, then vat together barrels from different areas.

sourmash The non-alcoholic, acidic residues left at the end of the first distillation of bourbon or rye is added to the mash of the next batch in the fermenter, making around 25 percent of the total liquid in that vessel. Also called "backset" and "setback," this acts as a souring agent and facilitates fermentation in the hard, limestone waters of Kentucky.

wash This is fermented wort at around 8% Vol, not unlike a strong, unhopped ale.

washback This is the vessel in which fermentation takes place. Washbacks vary in size and are traditionally made from Oregon pine (aka Douglas fir), and increasingly from stainless steel, which is easier to clean.

wash still The first still that is used in pot still distillation is the wash or low wines still. Here the alcohol and water from the wash is separated—alcohol having a lower boiling point than water.

wort After mashing the liquid which passes to the washbacks for fermentation is called wort—a sweet, sticky semi-transparent liquid—essentially unfermented beer (the same word is used in brewing and dates from c. 1000).

RAW MATERIALS

3-SECOND NIP
Whisk(e)y may be made
anywhere from any cereal,
but to be termed "Scotch,"
"Japanese," etc., it must
be distilled in its country
of origin, according to
the legal definitions of
that country.

3-MINUTE DISTILLATION
India is the world's largest
producer of whisky: Eight
of the top ten bestselling
whiskies in the world are
Indian (with Johnnie
Walker and Jack Daniels).
However, the vast majority
of "Indian whisky" is locally
made or bulk-imported
malt whiskies blended
with "Indian Made Foreign
Liquor" (IMFL), typically
distilled from fermented
molasses, rice, millet,
buckwheat, and barley.
Good though many Indian
whiskies are, they cannot
be sold as "whisky" in
Europe, since they are not
wholly cereal-grain spirits.

Malt whiskey, distilled anywhere
in the world, is made only from malted barley,
yeast, and water. In some countries, the malt
is dried over peat, which produces fragrant
smoke; occasionally it is dried over different
wood types. Scotch and Irish malts use distillers'
yeast; in Japan, brewers' yeast is added—as
it formerly was in Scotland. American distillers
believe the yeast strain enhances the spirit
character and go to extremes to preserve
the individual strains. The nature of the water
individual distilleries sourced was once deemed
key to the style of their spirit but this is now
doubted, though water temperature in the
condensers affects the spirit's texture. Scotch
and Irish grain whiskeys use mainly wheat,
sometimes maize. Irish pure pot-still whiskey
includes other cereals, usually unmalted barley,
with a little wheat, rye, and oats. "Blended
American whiskey" adds neutral spirit, made
from any available grains. To be named "Straight
bourbon/rye," the mash bill must contain at
least 51 percent corn or rye—usually far greater.
Canadian whisky comprises mainly corn, with
the addition of some rye and (occasionally)
wheat. Japanese whisky uses the same raw
materials as Scotch.

RELATED TOPICS
See also
WHAT IS WHISKEY?
page 16

IRELAND
page 96

BOURBON
page 98

CANADA
page 102

JAPAN
page 104

EXPERT
Charles MacLean

*The barley used for
malt whiskey must be
of high quality (capable
of germination), but
the variety is more
important for yield
than flavor.*

MALTING

The grain used for single malts

is exclusively barley, *Hordeum vulgare*. Whiskeys from other parts of the world may use different cereals such as rye, wheat, maize, or a combination. Historically distilleries grew their own barley or sourced it locally. As demand grew it was sourced from abroad and from England as well as from Scotland and Ireland. New barley varieties are continually being introduced, with a view to increasing the amount of alcohol they yield. The whiskey industry does not believe the variety influences the flavor of the spirit produced from it, although this is debated. Freshly harvested barley cannot be made into whiskey. Turning raw, hard seed into spirit requires it to be malted to access the starch within each grain and convert it into sugar. The grains are steeped in water for two to three days then spread out in a warm, damp environment to germinate for about a week. Once the seeds begin to sprout, germination is halted by drying the "green malt" in a kiln. If peat is burned at this stage, the whiskey will have a smoky character. The malt is then ground into grist and "mashed" with hot water to convert the starch into fermentable sugars.

3-SECOND NIP
Malted, kiln dried, and milled, barley becomes "grist" and is the base element of all single malt Scotch and pure pot still Irish whiskeys.

3-MINUTE DISTILLATION
Several different barley varieties are used in the production of single malts. For maximum extract, distillers need plump, ripe grains with plenty of starch and not too much nitrogen. Provided these requirements are met, the variety—and its provenance—matter less. The variety most Scottish distilleries once used was the evocatively named Golden Promise; today Optic, Decanter, and Chalice are strains favored for better resilience and disease resistance.

RELATED TOPICS
See also
MASHING
page 54

FERMENTING
page 56

BLENDING
page 66

EXPERT
Charles MacLean

Hordeum vulgare, *a two-row species of barley, grows in temperate climates around the world. The pagoda-shaped roofs of the malt kilns are a distinctive feature of many Scottish distilleries, although only a few remain operative, including those at Balvenie, Bowmore, Highland Park, Laphroaig, and Springbank.*

MASHING

The early stages of making whiskey—milling and mashing—are crucial for yield. The germinated and dried grain is milled to form a coarse grist. Mixing the grist with hot water activates the enzyme amylase, which converts the starch in the grain into sugar. The grist passes through the "mashing machine" where it is mixed with hot water. This "mash" then falls into the mash tun, a cast iron or stainless steel vessel of several tons capacity, fitted with stirring equipment and a perforated base, through which the liquid extracted from the mash may be recovered. In days gone by, stirring was done manually, with wooden paddles then with mechanical "rake and plough" stirrers that revolved around a central axle. Several distilleries still have these, but most now use Lauter tuns, adopted from the German brewing industry, which allow for more complete extraction of soluble sugars. Being gentler than traditional mash tuns, they do not disturb the bed of the mash, and make it easier to create clear wort, the sugary water that will be fermented. The husks and spent grains left after mashing is completed, called "draff," are fed to cattle.

RELATED TOPICS
See also
MALTING
page 52

FERMENTING
page 56

MATURING
page 62

BLENDING
page 66

EXPERT
Charles MacLean

3-SECOND NIP
"Mash" comes from Old English *masc*, *max*, and *miscian*, meaning "to mix," and it is first attested c. 1000 in relation to brewing, in the combination "mash-wort."

3-MINUTE DISTILLATION
All whiskey-makers understand the importance of getting the grist right, otherwise the amount of wort that can be extracted will be reduced, and so too will the amount of alcohol. Indeed, if the grist contains too much flour, it may turn into sticky porridge and choke the mash tun. In relation to flavor, cloudy worts make for a malty spirit, while clear worts allow more fruity and floral notes to emerge.

The husks and grains left over from the mashing process are known as "draff." This is rich in fiber, protein, and oil, and is used as a cattle feed.

FERMENTING

3-SECOND NIP
Whiskey is essentially distilled ale—think of it as beer without the hops.

3-MINUTE DISTILLATION
The length of time the wash is fermented plays an important role in the flavor of the ultimate spirit. The first—yeast or alcoholic, fermentation— is complete in about 48 hours but if the wash is distilled immediately, the spirit tends to have a cereal-like flavor. Leaving it to ferment for a further day or two reduces acidity and encourages the development of fruity/ floral characteristics.

To create an alcoholic ale, known as "wash"—or "beer" in America and Canada— the wort must be fermented. It is cooled and pumped into a fermentation vessel called a "washback" or "fermenter." Traditionally these were made from wood, usually larch, Douglas fir (also known as Oregon pine), or cypress (in the USA); many distilleries now have stainless steel fermenters. Yeast is added and after a couple of hours the yeast cells begin to consume the sugars in the wash, converting them into alcohol and carbon dioxide. Fermentation can become violent as the wash froths up the washback, the bubbles being broken by revolving rods or "switchers." After about 34 hours the wash settles down, the yeast cells die off, and there is a dramatic increase in bacteria (mainly *Lactobacillus*), which lower the degree of acidity in the wash and precipitate a secondary or *malolactic* fermentation. This stage is important for developing complexity and fruitiness in the spirit. Those distilleries that do not use malted barley as their base material, such as Scotch grain, American, and Canadian whiskeys, cook the cereals in the industrial equivalent of a pressure cooker to soften the starch, then add some barley malt to provide the enzymes that will convert it into sugar. Fermentation times for such whiskeys tend to be shorter.

RELATED TOPICS
See also
MALTING
page 52

MASHING
page 54

EXPERT
Charles MacLean

Although traditionally built from larch, pine, or cypress wood, many modern washbacks are now made from stainless steel instead.

POT STILL DISTILLATION

3-SECOND NIP
Distillation is the process that concentrates and purifies alcohol; the complex flavor of whiskey derives from the "impurities" that are left in the spirit.

3-MINUTE DISTILLATION
The purity and character of individual whiskeys depends upon the amount of contact the alcohol vapor has with copper: the more contact, the purer, lighter, and (some would say) less-characterful the spirit. Many factors govern this—the size and shape of the stills, how they are operated, the style of the condensers, etc. Continuous stills produce a much purer, therefore lighter, style of spirit than pot stills, and the same is also true of American hybrid stills.

Once fermented, wash is about 8% Vol, like strong beer or ale. It is pumped into the wash still, brought to the boil, and simmered to begin separating the alcohol and water—alcohol vaporizes at 173.1°F (78.4°C), water at 212°F (100°C). The resulting liquid, called "low wines" (about one-third of the volume of the wash and at 23% Vol) is collected; the residue, called "pot ale" is concentrated by further boiling for use as animal feed. Low wines contain a range of undesirable impurities that must be removed by further distillation in a second still. Copper is considered the best material for removing impurities from the spirit, which is why stills are made from this metal. Impurities tend to be found in the first and later runnings from the still (called "foreshots" and "feints"), so only the middle fraction of the run, "the heart," is saved for maturation. Its strength is around 70% Vol. The earlier and later fractions are re-distilled. The still operator's judgement as to when to start and stop saving spirit is guided by experience, varies from distillery to distillery, and is key to the unique character of the spirit made at each distillery.

RELATED TOPICS
See also
SPIRIT STRENGTH
page 20

MALTING
page 52

FERMENTING
page 56

CONTINUOUS DISTILLATION
page 60

EXPERT
Charles MacLean

Traditional pot stills are made up of a boiling chamber, where the mash is heated, a lyne arm, which transfers alcohol vapor to the condenser, and a condenser, which cools the transferred alcohol vapor.

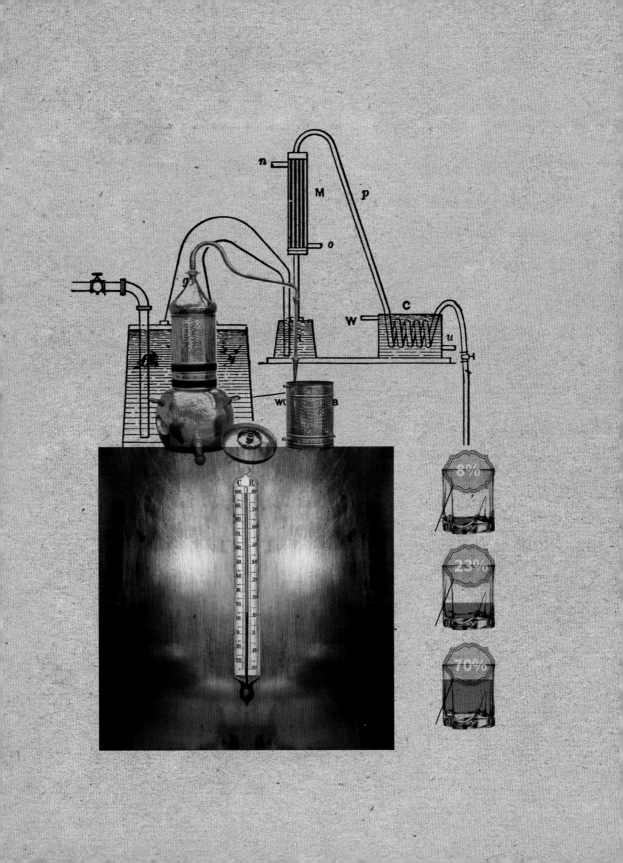

CONTINUOUS DISTILLATION

RELATED TOPIC
See also
POT STILL DISTILLATION
page 58

EXPERT
Davin de Kergommeaux

3-SECOND NIP
Preferred for making American, Irish, Scotch, and Japanese grain, and Canadian base whisky, continuous distillation produces consistent, lighter-flavored spirit quickly and economically.

3-MINUTE DISTILLATION
When French inventor Cellier Bloomenthal patented the first practical continuous still in 1813, he revolutionized the distilling industry. In 1828 a Scot, Robert Stein, unveiled his own continuous still, seemingly destined for success in Ireland and Scotland, until Aeneas Coffey introduced an improved version two years later. Some distillers made their own "patent" stills from wood, often calling them "Coffey stills." One such still operates at Diamond Distillers in Guyana.

Continuous distillation, like the simpler pot still, relies on the principle that water and alcohol vaporize at different temperatures. The earliest, nineteenth-century, continuous or "patent" stills comprised two cylindrical columns, the "analyzer" and the "rectifier," each divided internally into compartments by perforated copper plates. Unlike pots, column stills run continuously, producing very pure, high-strength spirit with less flavor and body. Cool wash enters the top of the rectifier, and descends via a serpentine pipe, where it is warmed by alcoholic vapor rising from the base of the column. The warm wash is then piped to the top of the analyzer and descends as liquid through its perforated plates. Steam pumped into the base of this column strips out the alcohol, causing the hot vapor to rise up through the plates. The vapor then returns to the base of the rectifier, and continues to rise until it meets a solid plate where it condenses and is drawn off as liquid. Flavor derives from the oxidation process inside the barrel in which the spirit matures. Economies inherent in continuous distillation significantly altered whiskey-making, leading to the creation of blended whiskey. A hybrid system (a rectifying column directly attached to a pot still), combining the processes in a single run, is common in America and Ireland.

Modern continuous distillation can involve several additional interlinked columns, which operate together much like a series of connected pots.

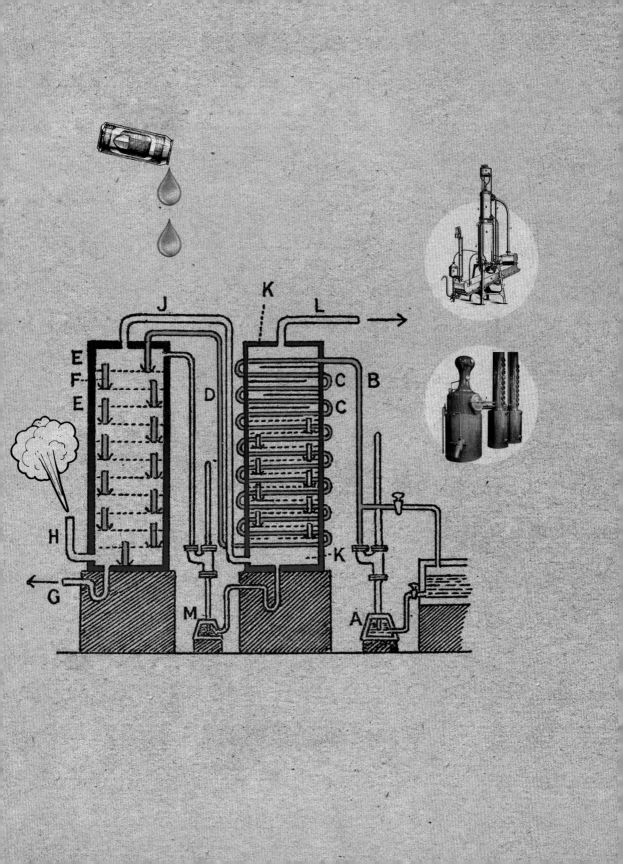

MATURING

The benefits of maturation were known at least from the 1820s. The requirement that the spirit must be matured for a minimum of three years before it can be called "whiskey" was only introduced in 1916 but has since been universally adopted, except in the USA, where two years' maturation is permitted. The favored casks were always oak—post-1990, this became the only wood allowed—and until 1946, when quantities of American oak ex-bourbon barrels became available, the majority were ex-sherry casks, used for transporting in bulk. In the eyes of most distillers, the first incumbent—bourbon, sherry, wine—seasons the wood, removing some of its more obvious characteristics, mellowing its impact upon the spirit. American distillers are the exception: Bourbon and rye must, by law, be matured in new wood—it is a key part of the whiskey's character. The cask is far more than a mere container; it adds desirable elements (including color—the spirit entering the cask is clear), removes undesirable compounds (especially sulfur notes), and, since oak-wood allows the spirit to "breathe," it interacts with the atmosphere and develops complex "mature" characteristics. The more times a cask is used the longer it takes to mature its contents. However, when they are deemed to be "exhausted," casks may be "rejuvenated."

RELATED TOPICS
See also
MALTING
page 52

FERMENTING
page 56

EXPERT
Charles MacLean

3-SECOND NIP
Whiskey must be matured in oak casks and in this "chrysalis," the spirit is metamorphosed from caterpillar to butterfly.

3-MINUTE DISTILLATION
The cask's interior must be toasted if it is to mature its contents. Toasting alters the structure and composition of chemicals immediately below the surface of the wood—for example, hemicellulose and lignin in the wood degrade with heat to produce desirable caramel, vanilla, and coconut flavors, which leach into the spirit. American barrels are then ignited, to line the interior with charcoal, which acts as a purifier by removing undesirable sulfur compounds from the spirit.

Since 1916, a spirit is required to be matured in oak for a minimum of three years before it can emerge from its cask as a whiskey.

1844
The claimed date of establishment of Whyte & Mackay Distillers

1881
The actual date when James Whyte and Charles Mackay set up their business, focusing on Scotch whisky, having previously worked for importer and merchant Allan & Poynter, which *could* trace its roots back to 1844

January 31, 1949
Richard Paterson born into a family that had long been associated with Scotch whisky

1966
Joins A. Gillies & Co.

1970
Joins Whyte & Mackay Distillers

1975
Appointed Master Blender by Whyte & Mackay Distillers

2013
Creates the world's most expensive set of whisky bottlings—The Dalmore Paterson Collection, given a $1,490,927 price tag by Harrods of London

2016
Celebrates 50 years in the Scotch whisky industry

RICHARD PATERSON

Richard Paterson is one of the most highly respected and experienced Master Blenders currently working in the Scotch whisky industry. Employed by Glasgow distillers Whyte & Mackay, he is often referred to with admiration as "The Nose," in reference to his exemplary ability to assess whiskies. Paterson is a third-generation blender, whose grandfather, William Robert Paterson, founded the family firm of Glasgow-based whisky blenders and bottlers W. R. Paterson Ltd in 1933. Richard Paterson's father, Gus, carried on the business, acting as a whisky "broker" or middle man, as well as blending and bottling in his own right.

Richard Paterson was introduced to the world of whisky at the age of eight, when he and his twin brother, Russell, were taken by their father to his Stockwell Whisky Bond in Glasgow where the company's casks were stored and where blending took place. He was shown the rudimentary aspects of nosing whiskies and finding words to describe their different characteristics. After this auspicious early start, Paterson's formal career in the whisky industry began in 1966, as an employee of the Glasgow whisky firm of Gillies & Co. Four years later he joined Whyte & Mackay Ltd, and within five years was their Master Blender.

With Whyte & Mackay, Paterson has worked not only with their well-known blends but also with their single malt portfolio.

During the last few years, he has created some remarkable—and at times remarkably expensive—rare expressions of The Dalmore, including The Dalmore Constellation Collection, comprising 21 whiskies distilled between the years 1964 and 1992, and The Dalmore Trinitas. Just three bottles of Trinitas were released, each containing spirit dating from 1868, 1878, 1926, and 1939, and one sold at Harrods' London store in 2011 for £120,000 (then $196,000). In 2013, a single 12-bottle set named The Dalmore Paterson Collection was offered for sale in Harrods for £987,500 ($1,490,927).

Increasingly, Paterson has adopted a high-profile role as an ambassador for the whiskies he has created, traveling extensively around the world to make his characteristically flamboyant presentations, which include throwing ice cubes around the room and setting off party poppers. Showmanship apart, he is admired, respected, and liked by hard-core whisky enthusiasts as well as novices and newcomers. He has an apparently encyclopedic knowledge of dates, an infectious passion for all things whisky, and for the subject of history, as well as a fondness for the finest Havana cigars. Paterson is opinionated, generous, and irredeemably Glaswegian (in a positive way). Time spent in his company is always memorable.

Gavin D. Smith

BLENDING

The gifted artisans who mingle distinct whiskeys from different distilleries, combining various flavor elements to create brands that convey consistent feel and flavor, batch after batch, are called blenders. An occasional smidgen of spirit caramel ensures constant color too. Scottish, Irish, and Japanese blenders mix richly flavorful malt whiskeys (and, in Ireland, pure pot-still whiskey), each exhibiting its own special characteristics, with mature grain whiskeys. Distilled to high ABV, grain whiskey mainly contributes flavors that develop in the barrel, and most importantly, mouthfeel—an often-unheralded quality. Blenders use a variety of malt whiskeys to bring smoky, fruity, floral, and other flavors to the blend. Balance is essential even if flavor is paramount. The most successful blends must taste like well-integrated units, not mixtures. Japanese distillers do not trade whiskies, making all the components for their blends in-house. In Canada, the once-common practice of trading whiskies among distillers declined dramatically in the 1980s. Today most Canadian whiskies, like Japanese, are best thought of as "single distillery blends." Richly flavored rye (or corn whisky) rather than malt whisky is used for Canadian blends, while American blends incorporate small amounts of bourbon into larger volumes of unaged neutral spirits.

RELATED TOPIC
See also
THE BLENDING HOUSES
page 116

3-SECOND NIP
The best blends, typically "greater than the sum of their parts," combine several different whiskeys to achieve balance, complexity, and richness rarely found in single casks.

3-MINUTE DISTILLATION
Distilling is no mere mechanical process, and blending overcomes inconsistencies that arise during distillation and maturation. Technically, even single malts are "blends" of a sort, mingling malt whiskeys from the same distillery. Straight bourbon is a blend of corn-based whiskeys, from different parts of tall rickhouses. But whiskeys *labeled* as blends combine several different types of whiskey, usually distilled in different distilleries. And "blended malts?" Malt whiskeys from various distilleries blended without including grain whiskey.

3-SECOND BIOGRAPHIES
WILLIAM EWART GLADSTONE
1809–98
British Chancellor of the Exchequer whose 1860 Spirits Act allowed blending of malt and grain whiskeys before excise duty had to be paid, and thus opened up the entire sector

HIRAM WALKER
1816–99
American entrepreneur whose practice of mingling newly distilled spirits before aging them, dubbed "barrel blending," is still used to make his Canadian Club whiskies

SAMUEL BRONFMAN
1889–1971
Canadian businessman who, in 1939 (after 200 attempts), finally combined more than 50 whiskeys to create the Crown Royal blend for King George VI

EXPERT
Davin de Kergommeaux

Master blenders need to be able to balance a wide range of flavors.

REGIONAL DIFFERENCES

coastal influences A catch-all term for saltiness, mineral notes, seashore aromas, Atlantic freshness, and other maritime olfactory aspects of a whiskey. Where such notes come from is hotly debated.

illicit stills In Scotland and Ireland before 1781, "private" distilling by a community was perfectly legal, so long as the whiskey was not offered for sale. After this date, all unlicensed distilling was "illicit."

Kildalton malts Kildalton is the parish in the southeast of Islay where Port Ellen, Laphroaig, Lagavulin, Ardbeg, and Caol Ila distilleries are located. They are sometimes referred to as the "Kildalton malts."

maltings The place where barley is turned into malt. Once invariably on-site at each distillery (the pagoda roof on the kiln has become the leitmotif of malt distilleries), these are now off-site, often in large, unlovely but essential buildings.

oily A tasting term to describe both a mouthfeel effect (palate coating) and an aroma akin to vegetable, olive, and machine oil; cream, candlewax, and unscented soap.

peaty Peaty aromas break down into "smoky" (lapsang suchong tea, smoldering sticks, beach bonfires, peat reek, tar, creosote; also smoked salmon, kippers, and smoked mussels) and "medicinal" (lint, Elastoplast, antiseptic, hospitals, dentists' mouthwash, iodine, liniment rub).

robust A descriptive term for a whiskey that is big-bodied.

tannic Mouth-drying, from the tannins (as in tea) in the oak casks in which the spirit is matured. European oak is more tannic than American oak.

terroir Literally the "earth": flavors derived from location. French winemakers attribute much of the flavor and idiosyncrasies of individual wines to this. Dave Broom, the distinguished whiskey writer, thinks of it more as "cultural terroir"—the craft that has been passed on at any distillery from generation to generation.

triple distillation Triple distillation, where the low wines from the wash still is re-distilled in two further stills, is today only employed at Auchentoshan, Annandale, and Springbank distilleries. The practice used to be more common, especially in the Lowlands.

waxy Tasting term used to describe both a mouthfeel/texture and an aroma reminiscent of candlewax. Highly esteemed and typically exemplified by Clynelish single malt, it used to be more common, before pipelines were so rigorously cleaned.

TERROIR

RELATED TOPIC
See also
RAW MATERIALS
page 50

EXPERT
Angus MacRaild

Terroir describes the character

of a product derived from environmental factors—geology, weather, geography. Though well-evidenced in wine, terroir is a subject of fierce debate in whiskey circles. For protagonists, local ingredients and certain environmental factors, such as proximity to the sea, establish "terroir" in whiskey. Opponents argue that production processes remove environmental subtleties. Origin of the cask, location, and duration of maturation also have a bearing, diminishing the potential for the land to exert an influence on a whiskey's final character. For the majority of Scotland's distilleries, the influence of terroir is unlikely; most source barley from multiple countries, use centralized maltings and disparate maturation locations. A more realistic relationship between product and place is that of what might be described as "transferred terroir." Traditionally, a whiskey's character was tailored by the individuals who made it, and they were informed by their relationship with the land on which they lived. As distilleries become increasingly technology-led, the environment's stamp diminishes. Terroir's influence (immediate or transferred) on the flavor of Scotch—though arguably once discernible—has since been rendered minuscule by the modernizations of production process and cask maturation.

3-SECOND NIP
Discernable differences in a whiskey's flavor define regional styles, but how much of that distinction is down to terroir—environmental influence—as opposed to the time-honored art and science of whiskey-makers?

3-MINUTE DISTILLATION
Advertising may evoke mist, moorland, and maritime influences on Scotch, and allude to makers steeped in tradition. Technological advances, however, allow modern-day distillers to dictate the flavor of their product. This shift has led to a resurgent effort by some distilleries to consciously re-connect their product to their terroir—Bruichladdich and Springbank for example. Both use local barley and have distinctive microclimates, elements of which, they claim, are revealed in their whiskies.

The very existence of terroir is controversial. Many argue modern technology renders any environmental influence on whiskey flavors negligible.

NORTH HIGHLANDS

The North Highlands is home

to some of the remotest mainland distilleries in Britain. Many predate functional road or rail networks, hence their frequent proximity to the sea in order to access the market. They are often fulsome malts, rich in personality with a distinctive coastal inflection. Many have become popular with enthusiasts recently, particularly Clynelish with its elegant waxy character and its peaty predecessor, Brora, beloved of collectors. Balblair and Old Pultney are well-balanced, fruit-driven whiskies with coastal freshness, the latter distinctly salty. The region's two most famous names are Dalmore, full-bodied and muscular, and Glenmorangie, one of the UK's bestselling malts, which is produced in the tallest stills in Scotland, making it unusually light for a Highland malt. The Singleton of Glen Ord is the bestseller in Taiwan, the world's leading malt-whiskey market, and is, like Clynelish, waxy and floral. The lesser-known Teaninich and Tomatin, both large-scale distilleries designed to create consistent product for blending, produce typically robust Highland-style malts. In recent decades modernizations in equipment, ingredients, and methodology have led to a slight taming of this "Highland" character, although many of these far-flung northern distilleries remain distinctive and idiosyncratic.

3-SECOND NIP
Full-bodied, waxy, oily, fruity, and displaying a frequent coastal influence, single malts from the Northern Highlands include some of Scotch whisky's most popular and vibrant characters.

3-MINUTE DISTILLATION
Brora Distillery was founded in 1819 by the Marquess of Stafford (later first Duke of Sutherland) as part of his project to "improve" his wife's vast estate—a project which involved clearing 15,000 tenants off the land to make way for sheep. The make was always highly regarded, and indeed "obtained the highest price of any single Scotch," but the distillery closed in 1983, due to the downturn in the whisky market.

RELATED TOPICS
See also
RAW MATERIALS
page 50

COLLECTING WHISKEY
page 130

3-SECOND BIOGRAPHY
GEORGE GRANVILLE
LEVESON-GOWER
1758–1833
Marquess of Stafford and first Duke of Sutherland who gained notoriety for his part in the Highland Clearances

EXPERT
Angus MacRaild

Whisky produced by Clynelish Distillery is a base spirit for the famous blend Johnnie Walker Gold Label.

WEST HIGHLANDS

Scotland's West Highland region is now somewhat malnourished for distilleries, although those that remain are bold, characterful malts encompassing several styles of generally high renown. Climatically this is one of the warmest and wettest regions and the maritime influence on its whiskies is abundantly apparent. Many distilleries are located near the sea, or are otherwise geographically isolated, a contributing factor to this region's comparative scarcity of producers. Campbeltown—home to three distilleries—was once a major region in its own right, producing fulsome, distinctly oily, and richly peated malts. Today Springbank is the epitome of the Campbeltown style. Glengoyne and Loch Lomond are lighter southern examples, although Ben Nevis or Oban would be the region's more emblematic names. In recent decades the West Highland characteristics have been somewhat softened by a combination of production modernization and the evolving requirements of blenders responding to the changing consumer palate which, from the 1960s, increasingly favored less pronounced peat. The region remains, however, firmly associated with an older style of whisky in which the predominant flavors are waxiness, coastal influences, fruitiness, and light smokiness.

Springbank, founded in 1828, is one of the three remaining distilleries in Campbeltown—once a major whisky region.

EAST HIGHLANDS

3-SECOND NIP
In whisky terms, the East Highlands is defined by a handful of distilleries with some of the true greats of Scottish distilling among its ranks, varied in style but often robust, occasionally exuberantly fruity, or gently peated.

3-MINUTE DISTILLATION
A natural environment for distilling, this relatively isolated corner of Scotland has plentiful peat bogs and farmland suited to barley growing so it is little wonder distilling flourished in the East Highlands. The levels of peat used in the malting process have been reduced over the years but the character of most of the whiskies remains muscular and punchy.

East Highland malts can be determined as a cluster of distilleries found on the "shoulder" of northeast Scotland between the triangle of Aberdeen, Peterhead, and Fochabers on the outskirts of Speyside. The definition of exactly which distilleries could describe themselves as "Speysides" was contentious for many years, and one, Knockdhu, is very much in the fruity-floral Speyside style. Sadly, some of the East Highlands' great distilleries are long-closed. Fine malts including mustardy and waxy Banff and lusciously fruity Glenugie are old-style examples that failed to survive the downturn in distilling during the 1980s. Traditionally East Highland malts were big, boisterous, and often peaty—although most, responding to the evolving tastes of the market, have tamed or lost their peat component. Only Ardmore remains as an illustration of this older style. Glen Garioch adds a wisp of smoke to a rich, fruity, and slightly gingery flavor-profile. It matures well in sherry wood, as does the mighty GlenDronach, which has deservedly won renown for its robust, sweet, and tannic whiskies, mostly drawn from ex-sherry casks. The lightest of the traditional East Highland malts are An Cnoc, from Knockdhu Distillery, and Deveron, from Macduff Distillery, both of which are malty and fruity.

RELATED TOPICS
See also
RAW MATERIALS
page 50

MATURING
page 62

SPEYSIDE
page 86

EXPERT
Angus MacRaild

Previous owners of GlenDronach Distillery have included Captain Charles Grant, the son of Glenfiddich founder William Grant.

CENTRAL HIGHLANDS

3-SECOND NIP

The "backbone" distilleries of the Central Highlands produce quaffable, post-dinner drams and are seen as the modern example of flavorsome Highland Scotch.

3-MINUTE DISTILLATION

With a plenitude of local peat and pure water, and ease of access to the barley grown on the east coast, many of these Central Highlands distilleries lie along well-worn tourist routes into the romantic mountains and glens of the Trossachs (made popular by Sir Walter Scott), or stretch, vertebra-like, close to the A9, the main road to Inverness and the north. As a result, they are among the most-visited distilleries in Scotland.

The Central Highland distilleries occupy a diagonal tract of mainly mountainous country between Stirling and Royal Deeside. Of all the Highland sub-regions, this disparate group of distilleries best reveals the "modern" interpretation of the Highland character: medium- to full-bodied malts, often fruity, with sweet-malty notes, sometimes lightly waxy, generally sturdy. Dalwhinnie, Scotland's highest working distillery, is probably the best-known name; full-bodied, sweet, with heather-honey notes. Aberfeldy has a similar but more biscuity and waxy profile. Both are classic examples of the Central Highland style. The most southern distillery is Deanston, robust and malty. The most northern, close to Balmoral Castle, is Royal Lochnagar—a complex character, redolent of linseed oil, pine, and hardwood shavings. Blair Athol, Glenturret, and Tullbardine, all in Highland Perthshire, are fulsome and well-balanced drams, starting sweet and finishing dry. Outside Pitlochry, Edradour, until recently the smallest distillery in Scotland, makes a lighter, more pear-like spirit, increasingly floral with maturation and often finished in ex-wine casks. The malts of this region prove to be "central" in character as well as location, being natural stepping stones between the more elegant Speysides and the more rugged Eastern and Northern Highlanders.

RELATED TOPICS

See also
NORTH HIGHLANDS
page 74

EAST HIGHLANDS
page 78

SPEYSIDE
page 86

DESCRIBING FLAVOR
page 146

3-SECOND BIOGRAPHY

SIR WALTER SCOTT
1781–1832
Scottish novelist for whom good Scotch was part of the romanticized vision of Highland culture that informed much of his work; many whisky brands are allied with either the author or his fictional characters

EXPERT

Angus MacRaild

Best known for his novels, plays, and poems, Sir Walter Scott was also a whisky afficionado who kept "plenty of right good and young" Highland whiskies in his cellar.

LOWLANDS

RELATED TOPICS
See also
NORTH HIGHLANDS
page 74

WEST HIGHLANDS
page 76

EAST HIGHLANDS
page 78

CENTRAL HIGHLANDS
page 80

EXPERT
Angus MacRaild

3-SECOND NIP

Persistently overshadowed, in more ways than height, by the stalwart Highlands, the Lowlands region nonetheless quietly produces mostly light, clean, crisp malts.

3-MINUTE DISTILLATION

Until recently, the lighter-style Lowland malts were not hugely popular, as the region's dwindling number of distilleries reflected. The new distilleries—Ailsa Bay, Annandale, Daftmill, Eden Mill, Glasgow, InchDairnie, and Kingsbarns—suggest a brighter future for the region once their spirits reach maturity or are released. Today the largest Lowland distilleries make grain, not malt, whisky. Cameron Bridge, Girvin, and Strathclyde produce millions of liters of grain whisky for blends, as well as neutral spirit for vodka and gin.

The Lowland region is Scotland's most "dis-spirited" whisky-producing district. Once there were distilleries in every sizable town; but this shrank to only three until 2005 when Daftmill opened, followed by five more after 2014. It might be claimed that the region suffered, historically, from an unfavorable comparison with the Highlands, an attitude that prevailed during the fledgling days of Scotland's whisky industry, when the Lowlands was home to some of the nation's earliest commercial distilling operations. Their malts were generally thought inferior to the illicit whisky of small Highland stills, although some "lost" distilleries, notably Rosebank and St. Magdalene, became very highly reputed. Lowlanders, traditionally considered to be the lightest of Scotland's malts, were often triple-distilled, which makes for greater purity and suitable aperitifs. Triple-distilling continues at Auchentoshan—a fruity, floral dram. The other leading Lowland malt is Glenkinchie, which, while fresh, citric, and fragrant, is full-bodied. The region's remaining long-established distillery is Bladnoch, Scotland's most southerly distillery, which despite a checkered career, is returning to full production: a "rural," grassy, citric malt of good character.

Although not as well-known historically as a whisky-producing region, the Lowlands in fact now produces a number of leading malts, from distilleries including Auchentoshan and Bladnoch.

December 19, 1839
Born in Dufftown in Banffshire, Scotland, to William Grant—nicknamed Old Waterloo—and Elisabeth Grant, née Reid

1859
Marries local girl Elizabeth Duncan, while working as a shoemaker

1864/65
Gives up shoemaking to become a clerk at Tininver, the local lime works

1866
Leaves job at lime works to become a bookkeeper for George Cowie at Mortlach Distillery in Dufftown

c. 1870
Attempts to start own quarrying business on Drummuir Estate fall through. Begins to consider distilling

1886
After two decades at Mortlach, uses his life savings to start building Glenfiddich with his family

December 25, 1887
Spirit flows from the Glenfiddich stills for the first time

1892
Signs purchase agreement for 10 acres down the road from Glenfiddich in order to build second distillery, Balvenie

1898
Creates Grant's Standfast Blended Scotch Whisky

1900
Suffers a stroke that will eventually cause him to go blind

1903
William Grant & Sons becomes a Private Limited Company

1908
Goes completely blind and begins working from bed, while his daughter Meta cares for him

January 5, 1923
Dies at home from 'old age' and is buried in the churchyard of the parish of Mortlach

WILLIAM GRANT

William Grant, the founder of

William Grant & Sons whisky distillers, was a man who went beyond the potential boundaries life had laid out for him. Born in Dufftown, Scotland, his childhood was typical for the time: attending grammar school in winter and herding cattle from the age of seven during the summer months. First apprenticed as a shoemaker, the early sign of Grant's true potential appears in 1864 when he decided to give up shoemaking and take a job in the local lime works—a radical move when most would have stuck with their apprenticed profession. A falling-out between the lime works owners saw Grant move to Mortlach distillery as its bookkeeper. Never one to sit still, he began planning his own quarrying business, even finding a partner, and a location to do so. Unfortunately, permission to quarry at Drummuir was pulled at the last minute. Despite this setback, he immediately began working on his next move, now investigating distilling. He was swiftly promoted to manager at Mortlach, and along with his wife's diligence, began saving as much of his $125 annual salary as possible to realize his ambition to build his own distillery—no easy feat when the couple's brood was on its way to expanding to nine children.

When another local distillery—Cardhu—decided to renovate, William approached its owner, Elizabeth Cumming, and purchased the old equipment for £119. Aged 48, he quit Mortlach and began building the Glenfiddich distillery himself, assisted by his children, on a site he had leased on the edge of Dufftown. Over 15 months, the family worked to lay the foundations, finally seeing the spirit flow from the stills on Christmas Day 1887. A chance opportunity with Aberdeen-based liquor wholesaler William Williams allowed the Grants to sell their output of 400 gallons of spirit per week, and expand the distillery site. When a potential rival tried to buy the site's adjoining land, Grant jumped in, securing the Robbie Dubh spring for the exclusive use of his distilleries, and built Balvenie distillery in 1892/3.

While many may have allowed financial success to go to their heads, Grant remained a committed community member, continuing his duties as a church elder and head of Dufftown Volunteers Band. In 1898 he developed the Grant's blended whisky brand, one that stands the test of time today. In 1900, he suffered a stroke, but continued heading the business, eventually expanding ownership to the whole family in 1903.

On William Grant's death he left a lasting legacy: Today, the internationally recognized company is run by the fifth generation of his descendants.

Alwynne Gwilt

SPEYSIDE

Speyside is the undisputed

capital of malt whisky production in Scotland. Relative to the Highlands the region is small, yet it includes nearly half of all operational distilleries, scattered throughout the Royal Burgh of Elgin, its proximate villages, the banks of the River Spey, and the uplands of Glenlivet. The whiskies are generally sweeter than other malts, and tend to fall into three broad styles: light and floral (e.g. Glenfiddich, Glen Grant, Cardhu, Linkwood, and Aultmore), medium-bodied (e.g. The Glenlivet, Aberlour, Cragganmore, Benriach, and Benromach), and robust (e.g. The Macallan, Glenrothes, Mortlach, Glenfarclas, and Balvenie). All are complex, fruity, and elegant; the last group benefits from maturation in ex-sherry casks, becoming rich and tannic with dried fruits and spice. Glenlivet was already famous for its (illicit) malts by the 1820s, and some of the earliest distilleries to take out licenses after 1823 are found in the region, but it was only after the opening of the Strathspey Railway that the district came into its own: 24 of the 40 distilleries built during the 1890s were on Speyside, most still in production. Many attached "Glenlivet" to their name as an appellation of quality.

RELATED TOPICS
See also
NORTH HIGHLANDS
page 74

WEST HIGHLANDS
page 76

EAST HIGHLANDS
page 78

CENTRAL HIGHLANDS
page 80

3-SECOND NIP
Almost half of Scotland's working distilleries are located in the Speyside region, including the world's bestselling single malts: The Glenlivet, Glenfiddich, and The Macallan.

3-MINUTE DISTILLATION
In 1820 it was estimated that there were 200 illicit stills in Glenlivet alone: It was the district's remoteness that attracted the smugglers, and the broader region's success was founded on the skills of these early distillers, and the fame of their malts. That, and the abundance of barley, peat, and pure water. A classic whisky text noted: "It would be no true—or, at least, no very discerning—lover of whisky who could enter this almost sacred zone without awe" (Aeneas MacDonald, 1930).

3-SECOND BIOGRAPHY
GEORGE SMITH
1792–1871
Founder of The Glenlivet Distillery with his son John Gordon Smith in 1824

EXPERT
Angus MacRaild

It was a case of poacher turned gamekeeper when illegal distiller George Smith obtained his first license to distill whisky at The Glenlivet Distillery in 1824.

ISLAY

RELATED TOPICS
See also
SPEYSIDE
page 86

OTHER ISLANDS
page 90

EXPERT
Angus MacRaild

3-SECOND NIP
An island of famous distilleries, their distinctive and evocative flavors of peat smoke, seashore, and medicine are adored around the world; even Islay's lighter examples are widely considered to be emblematic "coastal" whiskies.

3-MINUTE DISTILLATION
Islay can make a good claim to be the cradle of distilling in Scotland, and it is likely that the secrets of distillation were brought here from Ireland by a learned family of physicians named MacBeatha, who arrived in 1300 in the marriage train of an Irish princess. Succeeding generations of MacBeathas became hereditary physicians to the Lords of the Isles and the Royal Family.

Islay is the southernmost island of the Inner Hebrides. With eight distilleries, it is second only to Speyside as a "whisky capital" and its smoky malts enjoy worldwide celebrity. There are comparatively few trees on Islay and the earliest distillers needed fuel—this was supplied by peat, a composite of aged vegetation such as heather and sphagnum moss, dug from peat bogs, dried, and commonly used as fuel in the Highlands. Peatsmoke is highly fragrant and adheres to the green malt husks during kilning, giving the whisky a pronounced smoky/medicinal flavor. Nowhere are these flavors in greater evidence than the three southern "Kildalton" malts: Lagavulin (rich, sweet, fruity, fragrant), Laphroaig (pungent, medicinal, with carbolic and coal-smoke flavors), and Ardbeg (tarry, oily, reminiscent of beach bonfires). The island's capital is Bowmore, eponymous home to one of Scotland's oldest distilleries—its make is softer, floral, and fruity with wispy peat smoke. In the north near Port Askaig, the ferry link to the mainland, Caol Ila is sweet, maritime, and antiseptic; in the west is Kilchoman—Islay's newest distillery—sweet, salty, and ashy. The lightest malts on Islay are Bunnahabhain (light, fruity, and maritime) and Bruichladdich, full of lively green fruits, sweet malt, and Atlantic freshness.

Peat smoke gives the whiskies of Islay their characteristic flavor and aroma.

OTHER ISLANDS

Only a handful of nearly 800

islands off Scotland's mainland produce whisky, but they include some of Scotland's most "cult" distilleries ranging in style from soft but invigorating to powerful, peaty, and full-bodied. What they share is an evocative sense of their coastal locations—salty and maritime, with seaweed and iodine. Talisker on Skye is probably the most famous Hebridean malt; peppery and peaty with plenty of sea-air freshness. Further north is Orkney's Highland Park, which, with its balance of peat, heather-honey notes, and light fruits, deserves its reputation as a great "all-rounder." Orkney's second distillery, Scapa, is lighter with fruitiness and fresh malty sweetness. Mull's lone distillery, Tobermory, produces two single malts: The namesake is unpeated, cereal, lightly oily; Ledaig, its peated sibling, is smoky, oily, even kippery. Jura's eponymous malt is also oily, with pine sap, orange zest, and nuts, whereas the Arran malt is comparable to a light Speyside, with coastal notes. The most recent island distilleries are: Abhainn Dearg, on Lewis, a tiny one-man show, and Isle of Harris Distillery on the island of the same name, a community project that also makes gin. Although the whisky from Isle of Harris is not yet available.

3-SECOND NIP
Collectively, the island malts are all hallmarked by a coastal freshness and liveliness that unites their individual characters—some peaty, some rich, and some light and fruity.

3-MINUTE DISTILLATION
The natural romance of Scotland's islands has attracted interest from new distilling enterprises with distilleries planned or underway on Bute, Barra, Shetland, Skye, and Arran. Historically, distilleries were all close to the shore, since the only way to transport casks was by sea. This has led to the claim that their coastal location influences their whiskies' character. Though undeniably evocative in flavor, the science behind the whiskies remains hotly debated to this day.

RELATED TOPICS
See also
TERROIR
page 72

ISLAY
page 88

EXPERT
Angus MacRaild

Talisker, from the Isle of Skye, and the namesake whisky from the Isle of Jura are two of the most well-known spirits distilled on the Inner Hebridean islands.

NATIONAL DIFFERENCES

charcoal filtration Some whiskeys, such as Jack Daniel's, are "purified" by being filtered through a bed of maple charcoal. This process is also commonly part of vodka production.

congeners Flavor-bearing compounds that lend distinctive character to spirits or wine, by aroma or taste.

cooperage A cooperage is where casks/ barrels are made or repaired. Formerly all distilleries would have a cooperage on site; today distilleries mainly rely on centralized cooperages. Ninety percent of new Scotch whisky casks are from American cooperages, 10 percent from Spanish cooperages.

fillings Blenders traditionally fill their own casks with spirits they require for their blends, reciprocating with distillery owners by filling an equivalent number of casks at their own distilleries. Since the spirit cannot be named "whiskey" until it is three years old, it is referred to as "fillings."

fusel oils A mixture of several alcohols (chiefly amyl alcohol), produced as a byproduct of fermentation. The word derives from the German *Fusel*, meaning "bad liquor."

Hanyu Card Series In the 1940s Ichiro Akuto, whose family had been making alcohol since 1625 (sake, then shochu) opened a whisky distillery in the industrial town of Hanyu on Honshu, Japan's southern island. Alas, the whisky market in Japan collapsed in 2000 and Hanyu closed, leaving Akuto-san with 400 casks of maturing stock. This he began to release labeled with playing-cards. A full set of these (54 "cards," including two rare jokers) sold for $489,451 in Hong Kong in 2015.

mizunara maturation Japanese oak (*Quercus mongolica*) is also known as mizunara oak. Although rare, this type of wood has been used by the Japanese whisky industry since the 1930s and gives the whisky a unique set of flavors. The wood has extremely high levels of vanillins but is soft and very porous, making the casks made from mizunara oak prone to leaking and easily damaged. As a result, most Japanese whisky is mainly matured in either American oak (*Q. alba*) or European oak (*Q. robur*) and then transferred to mizunara casks to gain its flavorsome characteristics. Yamazaki is arguably the most accessible expression of the cinnamon spice flavor characteristic of Japanese oak.

Kentucky Bourbon Festival A week-long festival held in Bardstown every fall. It began as a simple bourbon-tasting dinner, hosted in 1992, and now attracts over 50,000 people from a dozen different countries to participate in more than 30 events. Other Kentucky towns and cities with strong bourbon affiliations include the state capital Louisville, Frankfort, and Lawrenceburg.

Kentucky Derby An annual horse race for three-year olds in Louisville, Kentucky. First held in 1875, it is the oldest horse-race in the USA.

new-make spirit The colorless spirit which runs from the still cannot be named whisk(e)y until it has matured for three years. It is simply "new-make spirit." Also referred to as "fillings."

rack/re-rack To rack is literally to "draw off wine, beer, or whisky" from any sediment that has accumulated in the cask. Re-racking whiskey is the transfer of the spirits into another cask, typically one that formerly held wine.

Taketsuru bottlings Masataka Taketsuru was "the Father of Japanese whisky." The whisky named after him has been released as a blended malt by Nikka in a non-age statement version, as well as in 17-, 21-, and even 25-year-old variants. It contains a high percentage of malt from Miyagikyo, with the remainder coming from Yoichi, and is aged on average for around ten years in a variety of different cask types, including some ex-sherry wood.

triple distillation Triple distillation, in which the low wines from the wash still are re-distilled in two further stills, is today only employed at Auchentoshan, Annandale, and Springbank distilleries. The practice used to be more common, especially in the Lowlands.

worm tubs Until the 1950s, most Scottish malt distilleries condensed their spirit in worm tubs, usually located outside the still-house wall. The lyne arm—the copper pipe connecting the head of the still to the condenser—enters an open bath of cold water (the "tub"), where it coils like a spring, gradually reducing in dimension. Since worm tubs afford less contact with copper, they produce a heavier style of spirit. They have largely been superseded by shell-and-tube condensers.

IRELAND

3-SECOND NIP
Like Scotch, Irish whiskey reaches across malts, blends, and single grains, but its signature style is the single pot still.

3-MINUTE DISTILLATION
Irish single pot still whiskey is made from a mixture of both malted and raw "green" barley malt and noted for its oily texture and gingery spice. This style is all about texture, so take a large sip—enough to get a feel for those viscous oils and resinous spices. Open your mouth and breathe out (without swallowing) for a burst of green barley spice. Diversity aside, you'll never be confused about the "Irish taste" again.

Irish whiskey is a protean dram.
While the drink has many well-branded "rules," such as triple distillation, there are exceptions to these and as the number of offerings continues to explode, the rule-breakers have quietly become the trendsetters rather than the traitors of the drink's identity today. Put bluntly, there are three overlapping Irish whiskey scenes. The first drink is the super smooth sip you're most likely to see—Jameson and Tullamore Dew are the names here. Gentle blends and fruity single malts; approachable, delicate, and clean. The second drink is modern, experimental, and eager to distance itself from the palatable precedents mentioned above—smoked malts, Cabernet-tinted single grains, and even blends finished in barrels seasoned with Irish stout matured in barrels seasoned with Irish whiskey... These are the tipples turning heads—Dublin's Teeling Small Batch, for instance. But there's also a third drink. Oily, full-bodied, and far older than the smoothies or the experimentalists, these cultishly hunted "single pot still" heavyweights harken back to the kind of Irish that once filled Victorian snifters. Pot-distilled from a mixture of malted and raw "green" barley (and, historically, other raw grains too), these lathery spice bombs, such as Redbreast and Green Spot, were once the uniquely Irish sister to the esteemed single malt.

RELATED TOPIC
See also
IRISH WHISKEY
page 34

3-SECOND BIOGRAPHY
BARRY CROCKETT
1948–
Master distiller of Jameson who kept single pot still whiskeys alive when the style was nearly replaced by blends in the 1980s and 90s

EXPERT
Fionnán O'Connor

Today there are three different Irish whiskey scenes, which range from gentle and fruity, to oily and full bodied, through to smoky and experimental.

BOURBON

The origins of bourbon production are the stuff of speculation. The whiskey-making settlement of Bardstown in Kentucky claims a distilling bloodline dating back to 1776, and has trademarked the phrase "Bourbon capital of the world." According to urban legend, the spirit was first made by Baptist preacher Elijah Craig who distilled in neighboring Scott County, ageing his product in charred white-oak casks which impart a rich color and a sweet taste derived from the wood sugars. Unlike rye whiskey, bourbon must contain at least 51 percent corn, and it is no accident that Kentucky and neighboring states partly overlie a limestone shelf, which provides limestone-rich soil ideal for growing high-quality corn. Limestone also produces pure spring water, free from undesirable minerals but containing calcium that aids enzyme action during the fermentation process of distillation. Bourbon is made either in a column still or a combination of pot and column stills. Woodford Reserve is the only bourbon in the world entirely triple-distilled in three copper pot stills. A minimum maturation period of two years is stipulated for what is termed "straight" bourbon. The world's bestselling brand of bourbon is Jim Beam, while among the other high-profile competitors are Buffalo Trace, Evan Williams, Four Roses, Maker's Mark, Wild Turkey, and Woodford Reserve.

3-SECOND NIP
The state of Kentucky is the centuries-old heartland of bourbon distilling and home to most of the great names in the business.

3-MINUTE DISTILLATION
Bourbon whiskey takes its name from Bourbon County in Kentucky. The county itself was named in reference to the French royal family of Bourbons, a gesture of gratitude for the aid of the French during the revolutionary war of the colonies against Britain. Whiskey-lovers are grateful, too, for the week-long Kentucky Bourbon Festival that is held in Bardstown each fall. Bourbon is also the drink of choice at another event—the annual Kentucky Derby.

RELATED TOPICS
See also
AMERICAN WHISKEY
page 36

CONTINUOUS DISTILLATION
page 60

TENNESSEE WHISKEY
page 100

3-SECOND BIOGRAPHIES
ELIJAH CRAIG
c. 1738–1808
Virginia-born Baptist preacher who founded a distillery in c. 1789

JOHN RITCHIE
1752–1812
Scottish-born Kentucky distiller and another contender for the title of patriarch of bourbon

BILL SAMUELS JR
1941–
Seventh-generation American Bourbon distiller who created Maker's Mark

EXPERT
Gavin D. Smith

Jim Beam, produced in Clermont, Kentucky, is one of the most popular bourbon brands.

TENNESSEE WHISKEY

Distilling in Tennessee can be

traced back at least to the eighteenth century and, by the late ninetenth century, it is claimed that no fewer than 700 distilleries were operating in the state. Tennessee's whiskey-makers, like their Kentucky bourbon counterparts, fell prey to Prohibition, except in Tennessee their problems began earlier, with the state being declared "dry" in 1910. Production did not resume for 28 years, with just two distilleries, those of Jack Daniel and George Dickel, reopening—Dickel's 25 years after repeal. Tennessee whiskey has the same composition as bourbon (by law both contain a minimum of 51 percent corn), and it must be matured in new, charred oak barrels. Recognized with its own classification in 1941, Tennessee whiskey, unlike bourbon, is filtered through charcoal. This process is recorded as being pioneered by one Alfred Eaton of Tullahoma, near Dickel's distillery, in 1825 but some sources claim charcoal filtration was being practiced up to a decade earlier. Allowing new spirit to leach through a thick layer of maple charcoal is believed to "sweeten" and smooth the whiskey by removing some of the by-products created during distillation known as fusel oils and congeners.

3-SECOND NIP
After Kentucky, the state of Tennessee is considered one of America's most notable distilling centers, and it is home to the world's bestselling whiskey, Jack Daniels.

3-MINUTE DISTILLATION
Charcoal filtration is known as the Lincoln County Process in reference to where it was first developed. It wasn't until 2013 that "Tennessee whiskey" gained its first legal definition within state law. Ironically, special dispensation had to be made for the Pritchard distillery, established in 1997, which, despite being situated in Lincoln County, has never used the Lincoln County Process. The law allows for two spelling variants—whisky (as favored by George Dickel) and whiskey (as employed by Jack Daniels).

RELATED TOPICS
See also
AMERICAN WHISKEY
page 36

PROHIBITION
page 40

BOURBON
page 98

3-SECOND BIOGRAPHIES
GEORGE DICKEL
1818–94
German-born émigré who entered the USA in 1844, where he began to retail liquor and ultimately was involved in operating the Cascade Hollow distillery whose whisky bears his name

JACK DANIEL
1849–1911
American founder of the Jack Daniel's distillery built in his birthplace: Lynchburg, Tennessee

EXPERT
Gavin D. Smith

George Dickel and Jack Daniel's are the two major Tennessee whiskey brands.

CANADA

3-SECOND NIP

Canadian whisky needs a wry sense of humor—despite its "rye" nickname, its flavors vary broadly as growing numbers of connoisseurs will grudgingly attest.

3-MINUTE DISTILLATION

Campfire tales and barroom logic, more than facts, comprise the lore of Canadian whisky. When the label says "Canadian Whisky," it might contain a drop of wine or aged non-whisky spirits, though never even a smidgen of neutral spirit, fruit juice, maple syrup, or other additions as some know-it-alls still insist. Instead, a dash of rye is used for flavoring a whisky style that, traditionally, was always made from other grains.

Despite Canada's vast footprint, there are no regional whisky styles. Whiskies from Alberta's three distilleries, Black Velvet, Highwood, and Alberta Distillers, differ more from each other than from Manitoba's Crown Royal, produced 750 miles to the east, or Ontario's Forty Creek, Wiser's, Collingwood, Gibson's, or Canadian Club, distilled three provinces away. To a butterscotch debut, with pepper on the tongue, and a refreshing grapefruit-peel finish, each brand adds unique fruity, spicy, herbal, and floral dimensions. Base spirit from corn (or sometimes wheat or rye), distilled to high ABV in towering column stills, matures in used barrels where air slowly transforms alcohol into complex flavors that new barrels would mask. Flavoring spirit made from rye, wheat, corn, or barley, distilled to low ABV in short columns and pot stills, matures in used and new barrels. This emphasizes flavors of the individual grain type, the yeast and those derived from wood. Blenders mingle mature whiskies from these two streams to create the complex spirit called "Canadian whisky," though nicknamed "rye." In the 1970s, when conglomerates owned most distilleries, they shared blending whisky. Today, each distillery usually produces all its component whiskies, effectively making most, though not all, Canadian whiskies single distillery blends.

RELATED TOPICS

See also
SCOTCH & NON-SCOTCH
page 18

CANADIAN WHISKY
page 42

3-SECOND BIOGRAPHIES

SAMUEL BRONFMAN
1889–1971
A poor Bessarabian immigrant who founded Seagram's global empire with Prohibition earnings, therby costing himself the seat he coveted in Canada's Senate

JOHN K. HALL
1949–
First-generation whisky-maker who founded Forty Creek distillery from scratch, kickstarting the 21st-century renaissance of Canadian whisky

EXPERT

Davin de Kergommeaux

Canadian whiskies are mostly single distillery blends, with the most well-known brands including Crown Royal and Canadian Club.

JAPAN

Japan's whisky history began less than a century ago with the founding in 1923 of its first single malt distillery, Yamazaki, now the bestselling Japanese single malt, owned by Suntory. Sweet, accessible, with subtle incense aroma and cinnamon spice characteristic of judicious *mizunara* (Japanese oak) maturation, Yamazaki has six pot stills of different sizes, two styles of fermentation vessel, and five types of cask, allowing the distillery, potentially, to make 60 different spirits. Hakushu, owned by the same company, is lightly smoky; unpeated and peated spirit are distilled then blended together. Yamazaki and Hakushu combine brilliantly with Chita grain in the exemplary blend Hibiki (meaning "harmony"). Unusually, some of the whisky in the 12-year-old is matured in plum wine casks. Yoichi, owned by Suntory rival Nikka, may be the most traditionally Scottish of Japanese distilleries—the stills are coal-fired and worm tubs contribute to the heavy, oily whisky. Ingenuity abounds, as ever, with peated and unpeated spirit being distilled from different yeast strains in various still shapes and sizes. Miyagikyo makes single malt and grain whisky. The former, light and fragrant, combining well with the latter and the bolder Yoichi in Nikka's world-class range of blends. This includes the attractively packaged Nikka Whisky from the Barrel and culminating in the great Taketsuru bottlings.

3-SECOND NIP

Japan, unlike Scotland, has no history of blenders exchanging new-make spirit ("fillings"); instead, producers have nedeed to be self-sufficient by making different styles of single malt.

3-MINUTE DISTILLATION

When the distillery his grandfather built was demolished, Ichiro Akuto rescued the last 400 casks from the wrecking ball. The whisky was re-racked into as many different cask types as Ichiro could source, resulting in the famed Hanyu Card Series. Ichiro has now set up a cooperage at his small but perfectly formed Chichibu Distillery. His cooper builds *chibidaru* (literally "small barrels") casks to accelerate the ageing of Ichiro's exceptional youthful single malt.

RELATED TOPICS

See also
JAPANESE WHISKY
page 44

MASATAKA TAKETSURU
page 106

3-SECOND BIOGRAPHIES

SHINJIRO TORII
1879–1962
Japanese pharmaceutical wholesaler who founded a drinks business that became Suntory, the world's third largest spirits maker

ICHIRO AKUTO
1965–
Japanese distiller of artisanal single malts, founder of the Chichibu Distillery

EXPERT

Marcin Miller

The Yamazaki Distillery was Japan's first. More recently, the Chichubu Distillery was founded by Ichiro Akuto in 2007.

une 20, 1894
Born in Takehara,
Hiroshima, Japan

1918
Arrives in Scotland
in December

1919
Undertakes
apprenticeships at
Longmorn (April)
and Bo'ness (July)

1920
Marries Jessie Roberta
"Rita" Cowan on January 8

1920
Apprenticeship
at Hazelburn in
Campbeltown in May

1920
Returns to Japan
in November

1923
Begins work for Shinjiro
Torii in June

1924
Establishment of
Yamazaki Distillery,
completed November 11

1934
Founds Dai Nippon Kaiju
(which later becomes
Nikka) at Yoichi in July

1940
Launch of first Nikka
whisky in October

1961
Death of Rita in January

1969
Sendai Distillery
constructed in May

August 29 1979
Dies aged 85

onal Differences

MASATAKA TAKETSURU

Few whisky distillers have a television series made about them; *Massan* is a 150-episode dramatization (first broadcast in September 2014) spanning 50 years of Taketsuru's extraordinary life. Born into a sake-brewing family at the tail end of the nineteenth century, Taketsuru traveled to Scotland in the aftermath of the First World War and enrolled to read organic chemistry at the University of Glasgow. As well as learning how to make whisky, he found time to court and marry Rita Cowan, whose life was perhaps even more unusual than that of her husband, living in Japan for 40 years at a time when foreigners were mistrusted.

While in Scotland, Taketsuru undertook apprenticeships at Longmorn, Bo'ness, and Hazelburn distilleries, living in Campbeltown during the last of these with Rita. The knowledge and experience gained first-hand in Scotland formed the basis of the Japanese whisky industry, of which Taketsuru is rightfully considered the father. His return to Japan roughly coincided with the desire of Shinjiro Torii (founder of Suntory, the biggest drinks company in Japan) to build Japan's first "proper" whisky distillery. Torii had the funds and Taketsuru was the only man in Japan with the necessary skills. A ten-year contract was agreed and Taketsuru, as manager, set about planning and building Yamazaki Distillery.

Although Taketsuru suggested Hokkaido as a suitable location, Torii decided to opt for the convenience of a location that was 10 miles (16 km) from Kyoto.

Thereafter, aged 40, Taketsuru fulfilled his ambition by establishing his own company and building Yoichi Distillery on the northernmost tip of Hokkaido; it looks like an attractive Scottish Highland distillery, right down to the remote location. Taketsuru's vision was to create whisky with an authenticity to match that of Scotland's finest. For many years Japanese chemists (including Taketsuru himself) had made ersatz versions of Western spirits but Taketsuru strived for integrity in the creation of whiskies in the traditional, Scottish way. He devoted his working life to achieving this goal, despite facing many obstacles, not least of which was that his first whiskies were maturing as the Second World War broke out and, obviously, the raw materials were in short supply.

The meticulous scientific rigor and attention to detail introduced by Taketsuru to Japanese whisky remains central to its global success. Fittingly, the single malts produced from Nikka's two distilleries are blended together to make Taketsuru; the 17-year-old expression was named World's Best Blended Malt in 2015.

Marcin Miller

ASIA & THE ANTIPODES

3-SECOND NIP
At the risk of sweeping generalization, what unites distillers beyond the classic homes of whisk(e)y is that they are not shackled by tradition.

3-MINUTE DISTILLATION
Accelerated aging may be a hallmark of other newcomers on the world whiskey stage. Lark Distillery near Hobart, Tasmania, the island's only licensed distillery for 150 years, produces a Classic Cask single malt using local Tasmanian barley and aged with alacrity in 100-liter casks (smaller casks have more spirit-to-wood contact, which results in a shorter maturation period).

The world of whiskey is expanding its horizons and, after Japanese, the next big thing to challenge Scotch, Irish, or bourbon may well be Indian, if not Taiwanese. India makes single malts using barley grown in the foothills of the Himalayas at Amrut, maturing its spirit largely in ex-bourbon casks under tropical conditions at Bangalore (3,000 feet/1,000 meters above sea level), while Goa's unutterably beautiful tropical coast is where Himalayan barley, traditional pot stills and warm temperatures combine to produce the very good, distinctive single malts of Paul John. And in 2015 a whisky from Taiwan made history when it was awarded the prize for being the best single malt: Kavalan, the first subtropical whisky distillery established in 2006, and the sole international player from the island nation, where the high temperatures result in speedier maturation and a concentration of flavors. As age statements start to disappear, reducing the number of years required to mature a single cask in a decade is all the more remarkable. This triumph is not an isolated instance but part of a growing trend for top-notch whiskeys to be successfully made in climates, latitudes, and sometimes at surprising altitudes alongside malt whiskey's historic homes of Scotland, Ireland, and North America.

RELATED TOPIC
See also
JAPAN
page 104

EXPERT
Marcin Miller

Asia and the Antipodes are home to a range of new single malt brands, including Lark from Tasmania, and Paul John and Amrut, both from India.

OTHER WORLD WHISKEYS

Beyond the Big Five (Scotland,

Ireland, USA, Canada, and Japan), whiskey is distilled in many grain-growing regions of all continents and climates. Wales has Penderyn and England has St. George's, Adnams, and Lakes Distilleries. Since the mid-1990s, whisky has been made throughout Europe, from different grains (rye, spelt, buckwheat, barley). Much is small-batch for local consumption, such as Blaue Maus from Germany, Roggenreith from Austria, and, more recently, Puni from Italy, and Flóki from Iceland. Whiskies, particularly malts, gaining international respect are made in Belgium (Belgian Owl, Goldlys), Denmark (Braunstein, Stauning, Fary Lochan), Finland (Teerenpeli), France (Glann ar Mor, Armorik), the Netherlands (Millstone, Frysk Hynder), Spain (DYC), Sweden (Mackmyra, Hven, Box), Switzerland (Säntis); and some are award-winners, for example Germany's Slyrs, the Netherlands' Millstone, and Sweden's innovative Mackmyra, which matures whisky in many different casks, among which are ex-lingonberry wine casks. China announced its Wenzhou Distillery and Russia is building a distillery near St. Petersburg, though neither has released any products yet. South America too is on the malt-whiskey map with Union Distillery in Brazil and La Alazana Distillery in Argentina, while the South African Distell Company produces single malt and grain whiskies: Three Ships and Bain's.

3-SECOND NIP
Whiskey is now made around the world, in places with a ready supply of grain, pure water, yeast, and power.

3-MINUTE DISTILLATION
Some East European countries claim to make whisky but purchase it elsewhere and bottle it locally, such as Black Ram, from Bulgaria. The Czech Republic may be the exception to the rule; the Gold Cock distillery boasts it has produced an eponymous whisky since 1877. The spirit comes in two versions but is seldom seen outside the Czech borders. Turkey used to make Tekel whisky in a government-controlled environment (*tekel* means "monopoly" in Turkish).

RELATED TOPIC
See also
ASIA & THE ANTIPODES
page 108

EXPERT
Hans Offringa

Whiskey is now made in many countries which, in Europe at least, tend to be those with traditions for distilling brandies, eaux-de-vie, and aquavit vodkas.

THE WHISKEY TRADE

age statement If a bottle states its age on the label, this is the minimum length of time its contents have spent maturing. Once whiskey is bottled at a certain age, it remains that age forever. A ten-year-old whiskey bottled in 1960 is still, and always will be, a ten-year-old whiskey. Older age statements are generally rarer and more sought after by collectors and investors. At the time of writing, the oldest Scotch whisky ever bottled was a 75-year-old, bottled in 2015. That particular whisky had matured in an oak cask for a staggering 75 years; however, now it is in glass rather than a cask, it will always be a 75-year-old.

Blair Castle The seat of the Dukes of Atholl, Blair Castle, is also the headquarters of the Keepers of the Quaich, the whisky industry's most prestigious "club." Founded in 1988 it serves to honor individuals who have made a significant contribution to the prestige and success of Scotch whisky worldwide.

cask strength Literally the strength the whiskey is at when it is bottled without dilution with water, typically between 50%ABV and 60%ABV. Casks are traditionally filled at 63.5%ABV (111° proof) and the whiskey loses strength during the course of its maturation, and is commonly bottled at 40%ABV or 43%ABV. "Cask strength" is not defined in law, and the term is sometimes used simply to describe a high-strength whiskey.

chill-filtration When high-strength whiskey is chilled it can go slightly cloudy, owing to fatty compounds or lipids in the liquid precipitating. This can be off-putting for consumers, so most whiskey is now "polished" on the bottling line by reducing the liquid's temperature to around freezing and pressing it though a filter, which catches the lipids. Connoisseurs know, however, that these elements are big contributors to flavor, and especially texture, and are best left in.

date distilled/vintage This is the date an individual whiskey was distilled. In most cases, a vintage is not declared, but if it is, all the whiskey in the bottle must be from that year. In a small number of bottlings (mainly single cask/ultra-limited bottlings) the exact day/month/year is quoted. An old vintage can still be a "young whiskey" however: Whiskey distilled in 1950 could have been bottled as a ten-year-old after spending a decade maturing in a cask. When whiskey is bottled at a declared age, it remains that age forever.

La Maison du Whisky The leading French retailer was established in Paris in 1956 by Georges Benitah and is owned and managed today by his son, Thierry.

NAS expressions Whiskeys not declaring their age are termed No Age Statement bottlings. The term "expression" describes any bottling—thus, if an individual malt is bottled at NAS, 12, 18, 21, and 25 years old, cask strength, and wine-finished, seven expressions are available.

quaich Derived from *cuach*, the Gaelic for "cup," a shallow drinking vessel with two or more "lugs." The shape is reputed to have been inspired by a scallop shell. Early quaichs were made from staves of wood, later embellished with silver bands; today, most are made from silver or pewter.

silent distillery A distillery which has been temporarily closed or "mothballed" but is capable of resuming production.

under bond Whiskey held in a duty-free warehouse or shipped before duty has been paid.

vatting The mixing of whiskeys, typically of malt whiskeys from different distilleries, which gave rise to a "vatted malt," "pure malt," or a "straight malt." All these terms were replaced by "blended malt" under the Scotch Whisky Regulations 2009.

vertical tasting A tasting of several expressions of the same whiskey at different ages.

wine finishing Where the whiskey has been transferred into a cask that formerly contained wine (usually port or oloroso sherry) for the final year or two of its maturation.

THE BLENDING HOUSES

3-SECOND NIP
Blending different whiskeys, designed to appeal to a broad market, achieves a consistent product that can be branded. It created the global industry of today.

3-MINUTE DISTILLATION
Before the 1880s, Irish whiskey sold between three and five times as much Scotch in both Scotland and England, since it was perceived as being lighter and more consistent. The leading Irish whiskey houses—John Jameson, William Jameson, John Power, and George Roe—scorned the column still and published a polemic against blending in 1878. But in time they too became blenders.

Different whiskies have been mixed by spirits merchants and publicans since at least the 1820s, especially after 1830 when cheap patent-still grain whisky became available. In 1853, vatting malts before duty had to be paid was permitted. One of the first to take advantage of this was Andrew Usher & Co., Edinburgh agents for The Glenlivet, who created the first branded whisky, Usher's Old Vatted Glenlivet. When a further Act of Parliament in 1860 permitted the mixing of malt with grain whiskies under bond, this became a true blend, and many companies that remain household names followed Usher's example. Matthew Gloag offered blended whisky in his Perth shop by 1860, the year John Dewar employed his first sales rep; Arthur Bell attempted, unsuccessfully, to enter the London market with two blends in 1862; Alexander Walker, son of Johnnie, registered his Old Highland Whisky in 1867. Following the devastation of the French vineyards by the aphid phylloxera, blended Scotch replaced cognac as the English middle classes' drink of choice. By 1900, three companies predominated: Walker, Dewar, and Buchanan. In Canada, Joseph Seagram and W. P. Wiser were exploring blending and Hiram Walker was looking at blending the spirits before maturation, although Irish and American whiskeys remained unblended at this time.

RELATED TOPICS
See also
THE HISTORY OF SCOTCH
page 30

CONTINUOUS DISTILLATION
page 60

BLENDING
page 66

CANADA
page 102

3-SECOND BIOGRAPHIES
DAVID STEWART
1945–
Joined William Grant & Sons in 1962; appointed Malt Master and Master Blender in 1974. Awarded an MBE for services to the whisky industry in 2015

COLIN SCOTT
1949–
Appointed Master Blender at Chivas Bros in 1989, having served a 16-year apprenticeship under the previous Master Blender, Jimmy Lang

EXPERT
Charles MacLean

The blender's art is to consistently create a whiskey with the flavor profile of the brand.

INDEPENDENT BOTTLERS

Single malts are not always

released by the company that distilled them; they may also be bottled and sold by third parties. Blenders must have a market for disposing of surplus casks or making up the shortfalls, so a secondary market in casks exists to satisfy this demand. Independent bottlers can feed off the fringes of this pool, bottling up casks under their own label, usually naming the distillery. Brand-owners generally dislike the loss of quality-control, branding, pricing, and housestyle this implies, but with rare exceptions quality remains high. What's more, these renegades offer interesting variations on proprietary bottlings and have driven the shift to more natural bottling, without cosmetic processes like chill-filtration (to prevent haze when water is added) or artificial coloring with spirit caramel, added to burnish whiskey with the gleam drinkers are deemed to expect. Throughout the 1970s and 80s, "Indies" like Gordon & MacPhail and Cadenheads were the only source for malt fans looking to explore makes from distilleries whose entire output was otherwise destined for blends. The recent surge in demand for whiskey—from all five leading producing countries—has made it difficult for Indy bottlers to obtain good casks. As a result, many have built or acquired distilleries in order to barter with established producers.

3-SECOND NIP
Independents bottle single malts from distilleries they do not own under their own label, usually as single casks or very small batches.

3-MINUTE DISTILLATION
The reputation of an "Indy" is built on its cask selection. The best companies have a knack of finding the hidden gems that slipped through the cracks of the industry, and have the courage not to bottle the big boys' rejects. Some Indy bottlers, notably Compass Box, use their independence to stretch boundaries and explore flavor imaginatively.

RELATED TOPIC
See also
THE BLENDING HOUSES
page 116

EXPERT
Arthur Motley

Adelphi Distillery is among the most rigorous of cask selectors. Their releases now sell out so fast you have to be quick to buy any bottles. They know spirit and understand maturation, and also have a great nose for when a malt is ready.

THE KEEPERS OF THE QUAICH

Inspired by the ancient French wine guilds, such as the Chevaliers du Tastevin and the Commanderie de Bordeaux, the Keepers of the Quaich was founded in 1988 by the leading distillers of the day to honor those who had made a significant contribution to Scotch whisky. The Society has only ever inducted 2,549 members from over 100 countries. It has its own coat of arms, motto—*Uisgebeatha gu Brath*, "Whisky for Ever"—and tartan, all granted by Lord Lyon, King of Arms, and has its headquarters at Blair Castle, where it holds biannual banquets to admit new Keepers and Masters. Guest speakers at the banquets have included HRH The Princess Royal, HRH The Prince of Wales, HSH Prince Albert II of Monaco, Sir Jackie Stewart, Dame Stella Rimmington, Ronald Reagan, F. W. de Clerk, and Alexander McCall Smith. The Society's patrons include the Dukes of Argyll, Atholl, and Fife, the Earls of Elgin, Erroll, Dalhousie, and Hopetoun, and Viscount Thurso. The Grand Master is head of the Society. The Management Committee is made up of representatives from each of the founding companies and membership is by invitation only, candidates being proposed by existing members.

RELATED TOPIC
See also
THE SCOTCH MALT WHISKY SOCIETY
page 124

3-SECOND BIOGRAPHIES
JAMES ESPEY
1943–
The Keepers was inspired by James Espey OBE, when he was appointed Deputy MD of United Distillers (now Diageo)

THE RIGHT HON. THE EARL OF ELGIN & KINCARDINE KT
1924–
The Keepers' third Grand Master, who played a key role in combining dignity with humor

EXPERT
Charles MacLean

The Grand Quaich was commissioned by the Society as the centerpiece of its "regalia." It measures 24 inches (60 cm) across, is made from solid silver, and stands on a base of burr elm.

BOOM & BUST

Because whiskey as a commodity is highly unusual in requiring a minimum period of several years between production and public sale, distillers require something of a crystal ball to predict what levels of sales will prevail five, ten, and even 20 years down the line. So it is that there have always been periods of boom and bust, with either not enough whisky to go around, or a glut of spirit flooding the market. In terms of Scotch whisky, the second half of the nineteeth century saw a great period of boom, fueled by the apparently insatiable demand for blended Scotch around the world. New distilleries were built and existing ones modernized and expanded, and ultimately supply far exceeded demand. The bubble burst with the collapse in 1898/99 of the distilling and blending company Pattisons Ltd, which had been trading fraudulently, followed by a period over half a century long of whisky recession. The 1960s and 70s saw the next Scotch whisky boom, principally due to rising demand from the USA, but overproduction once again bedeviled the industry, leading the UK's largest distiller—The Distillers Company Ltd (DCL)—to close no fewer than 23 malt distilleries in 1983 and 1985.

RELATED TOPIC
See also
THE BLENDING HOUSES
page 116

EXPERT
Gavin D. Smith

3-SECOND NIP
Being a commercial activity that is reliant on market forces, each country's whiskey industry is prone to periods of boom and bust as global economies expand and contract.

3-MINUTE DISTILLATION
Boom returned to the world of Scotch whisky once more during the early years of the twenty-first century, with exports peaking at a value of £4.3 billion in 2012 (then almost $7 billion), representing a remarkable rise of 87 percent over a decade. As in the past, new distilleries were built by the industry's major players and many existing plants saw increases in efficiency and capacity. However, exports have fallen back slightly since 2012, and most distillers are viewing further expansion plans with a degree of caution.

The whiskey market has always been in a state of flux. Today, with new distilleries opening around the world, it is difficult to predict what the future might hold for the whiskey trade.

THE SCOTCH MALT WHISKY SOCIETY

RELATED TOPIC
See also
THE KEEPERS OF THE QUAICH
page 120

EXPERT
Charles MacLean

3-SECOND NIP
The SMWS is one of the world's premier whisky clubs, offering its members access to a wide selection of single-cask whiskies.

3-MINUTE DISTILLATION
Whisky-devotees join this Society to delight in indulging their passion for exceptional single malts in the company of like-minded individuals. All the malts on offer are rigorously selected by The Tasting Panel and bottled straight from the cask. North America is the Society's biggest market outside the UK but interest is fast expanding in Taiwan, Japan, and China.

"The Society" began in the late 1970s when Phillip "Pip" Hills discovered the joys of single-cask Scotch malt whisky, bottled at cask strength and without chill-filtration, which connoisseurs find detrimental to both the flavor and texture of their dram. He shared his experience with university friends and in 1978 they formed an informal group to buy, bottle, and enjoy single casks. This became a private members' club in 1983 when a historic, but derelict building—The Vaults in Leith, Edinburgh, dating from the twelfth century—came up for sale. It was purchased and restored, providing a Members' Room, Tasting Room, and offices for the nascent Society. Since then membership has grown to around 28,000 people, with franchised branches in 16 countries; a Members' Room opened in London in 1996, and a second venue was acquired in Edinburgh's New Town in 2004. That year the Society was acquired by Glenmorangie plc, but returned to private ownership in 2015. Membership is international and open to all upon payment of an annual fee, which entitles access to the Society's venues, the opportunity to buy the limited single-cask bottlings (currently around 450 a year, from 132 distilleries), to receive the club's quarterly magazine, and to participate in the Society's many tasting events around the UK and overseas.

The Vaults in Leith, Edinburgh, were originally used as a wine store before they were purchased by The Scotch Malt Whisky Society.

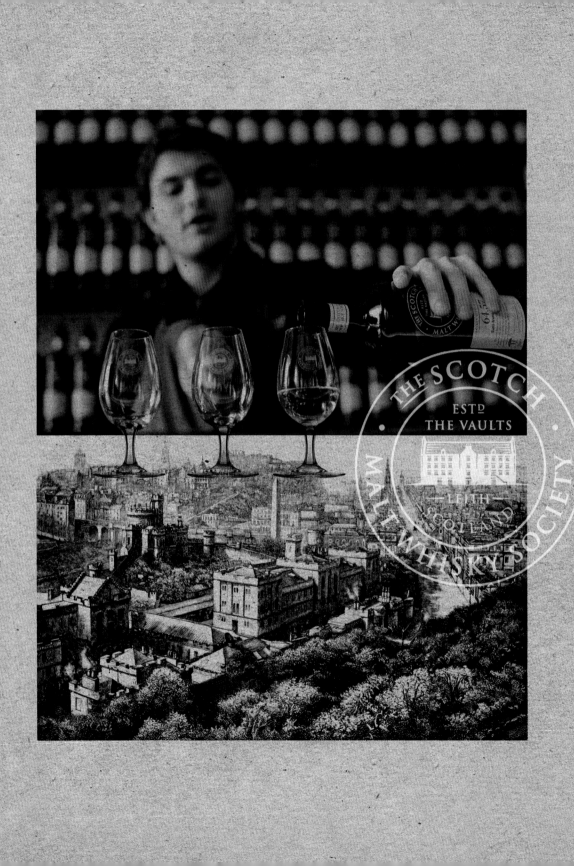

March 2, 1968
Born in London, the first son of Narinder Singh Sawhney and Bhupinder Kaur Sawhney

1971
Parents' grocery opens in Hanwell, west London

1990
Attends first whisky auction in Scotland

1991
Graduates from City University, London, and begins working full-time in parents' shop

1991
Relaunches his parents' shop as "The Nest" to great success

1992
The Nest named "Off-Licence" (liquor store) of the year, a remarkable feat for a small independent outlet

1998
Parents retire and sell their shop

1999
Founds The Whisky Exchange online with brother Rajbir

2000
Launches first independent bottling, a 1969 31-year-old Glen Grant

2005
Opens first retail outlet in London at Vinopolis in London Bridge

2006
Launches the Elements of Islay range of bottlings

2009
Launches the Port Askaig range of bottlings

2009
First Whisky Show festival launched at London's Guildhall

2014
Sukhinder and Rajbir listed among Britain's top 100 entrepreneurs of the year

2015
Launches Whisky.Auction, a dedicated online whisk(e)y auction company, and opens a new flagship shop in London's Covent Garden

SUKHINDER SINGH

Sukhinder Singh is one of the world's foremost whisky collectors and co-owner of The Whisky Exchange (TWE), a company that has grown to dominate modern whiskey retailing. He is also recognized as a leading authority on whisky and a passionate promoter of Scotch. From an unexpected start managing his parents' liquor store in the early 1990s Sukhinder and his younger brother, Rajbir, have steadily forged a business that encompasses retailing new releases, old and rare bottlings, independent bottlings under his own labels and brands, wholesaling, specialist whisky festivals, and auctioneering.

Sukhinder's parents founded a grocery in 1971 in Hanwell, west London. It proved a formative environment; from an early age Sukhinder became interested in the miniatures that his parents stocked and enjoyed talking with their regular customers who would come in to buy single malts, a product few London grocers stocked at the time. His first forays into collecting were in whisky miniatures, of which he acquired over 700.

In 1991 he graduated with a degree in Chartered Surveying. It coincided with one of London's worst property crashes so instead he took on his parents' shop, expanding the business and including more whisky. Their new shop, "The Nest," opened in 1991 attracting a loyal following.

At the same time Sukhinder began to attend whisky auctions at Christie's in Glasgow and to collect whisky more seriously. Throughout the 1990s his connections with collectors and whisky enthusiasts in Japan and Europe multiplied and he became gradually more immersed in the world of serious whisky appreciation and collecting.

When Sukhinder and Rajbir's parents retired in 1998, the brothers wanted to focus fully on the whisky business. Narrowly rejecting the idea of a shop in central London they decided to take the online route. A website was built by Rajbir's friend and a small warehouse space was acquired. Within two days they were getting orders. From here the business—and Sukhinder's collection—continued to grow. Today TWE offers one of the world's largest selections of old and rare bottles with over 4,000 products in stock including single malts, blends, and numerous other fine spirits. Over the years they have also increased their own bottlings and brands, released under labels such as Malts of Scotland, The Whisky Society, Port Askaig, and Elements of Islay. In 2015 TWE opened a new flagship retail shop in London's Covent Garden offering an extensive range of champagnes, wines, and craft beers alongside whiskies and other fine spirits.

Angus MacRaild

SPECIALIST RETAILERS

3-SECOND NIP
A specialist whiskey merchant thinks little of carrying more than 300 whiskeys at any one time, with a constantly rotating stock aided by the extended reach of web-retailing.

3-MINUTE DISTILLATION
Securing a good relationship with a specialist retailer is essential for those wanting to build an interesting collection. Similarly, discerning whiskey-drinkers are more likely to secure sought-after releases by buying their regular drinking stock from the same shop, rather than seeking out the cheapest supermarket deal.

Specialist merchants have had a key role in the appreciation of malt whisky latterly, and an even bigger one in the blenders' story. Premium blends such as Ballantine's, Chivas, Johnnie Walker, and The Famous Grouse were all created in the cellars of licensed grocers' shops. Specialist whisky shops began to appear in the second half of the twentieth century with a revival of interest in single malts. La Maison du Whisky in Paris was founded in 1956, and Milroy's of Soho began to focus on whisky in the 1970s, initially with only four brands. Edinburgh's Royal Mile Whiskies opened in 1991, followed a year later by Loch Fyne Whiskies in Inveraray, Argyll, two of the first to sell online. Supermarkets and travel-retail outlets have sometimes provided amazing bargains as the industry chased volume, but as the whisky loch of the 1980s emptied, the focus shifted to exclusive ranges awash with No Age Statement (NAS) expressions. Everything changed in the 1990s with the rise of online retailing, and dedicated web-retailers such as the comprehensive Whisky Exchange and irreverent Master of Malt joining the digital offering from traditional shops. Web-retailing enables specialists to thrive in very remote areas; arguably it has also changed the way distillers release their whisky, with a proliferation of PR-led, story-based limited editions designed for rapid online sale.

RELATED TOPICS
See also
THE HISTORY OF SCOTCH
page 30

COLLECTING WHISKEY
page 130

3-SECOND BIOGRAPHY
EDOARDO GIACCONE
1928–96
Italian whiskey aficionado who opened the first whiskey bar and shop on Lake Garda, Italy, in 1958; he is recognized by the *Guinness Book of Records* as the first collector of whiskey, with 5,502 different bottles—excluding his trading stock

EXPERT
Arthur Motley

Whiskey traders have also taken advantage of online retail's rise in popularity.

COLLECTING WHISKEY

Humans display a passion for hoarding. We hoard all kinds of "stuff," and bottles of whiskey are no exception to this desire to acquire, keep, and often show off tangible assets. Arguably, serious whiskey collecting started in Italy some years ago. In the 1970s and 1980s Italy realized it could corner the market for *really* good Scotch. Vast quantities of the finest drams on earth were exported exclusively to Italy as most of the rest of the world was barely aware of "single malt Scotch." Many of these bottles were consumed, but many also went into collections. Fast-forward to the present day and the collectors' market has exploded as a global subcategory success story as rare and increasingly valuable bottles become ever more sought after. Whiskey producers actively target collectors with myriads of limited editions, rare releases, and vintage verticals. The reasons for collecting are seemingly limitless—some collectors want a bottle from every distillery, some want every bottle from a single cherished distillery, some collect birth year vintages, some collect as an investment, and others stock up on rare releases for future enjoyment.

RELATED TOPIC

See also
INVESTING IN WHISKEY
page 132

3-SECOND NIP

Stamps and coins are well-known collectables with established markets, but whiskey is turning into the collectors' darling as rare bottles become cherished belongings.

3-MINUTE DISTILLATION

It was only a matter of time before fakes appeared. Valuable bottles are relatively easy to refill and re-seal convincingly—in some countries there is a roaring trade in empty bottles. Clever forgers mock up old labels and auction "antique" bottles. In May 2016, a fake purported to be a bottle of Laphroaig bottled in 1903. The real thing would have been worth a small fortune. The rule of thumb is: If it looks too good to be true, it is. Caveat emptor.

3-SECOND BIOGRAPHY
VALENTINO ZAGATTI
1931–
Italian whisky collector who sold his world-famous collection of 3,013 bottles for an undisclosed sum said to run into millions of pounds

EXPERT
Andy Simpson

Whiskey bottles come in all shapes and sizes. Some collectors are more interested in the bottles they buy, whereas others are more interested in the contents within.

SPRINGBANK
CAMPBELTOWN MALT
50

65

1964

The
MACALLAN
Anniversary Malt
50

MacPhail's
50

WELSH WHISKY
100

INVESTING IN WHISKEY

Let's start by stating the

obvious: Whiskey is a drink; its very reason for existence is to be consumed; but for certain bottles, keeping them closed can reap financial rewards. Some of the rarest, oldest, best-quality bottles of whisky have, in some cases, seen stratospheric increases in value. Limited editions and commemorative bottles from iconic brands have been known to double or triple in value overnight (Macallan, Balvenie, Ardbeg, Dalmore, Lagavulin, and Laphroaig are good examples). Where no more spirit can be distilled, bottles from closed distilleries are increasingly rare and in demand. Port Ellen, Brora, and Rosebank are among the big "silent" names. Vintages (date distilled) from long ago and old age statements are also ferociously sought after with only the best-quality spirit making the grade—one person's investment today can be another's favorite drink tomorrow. Traditionally limited to Scotch, the recent market has also seen significant increases in value for rare bottles of Japanese whisky and American whiskey. Canny investors only buy full sealed bottles—casks are a risk too far as they can leak and there's no guarantee they turn out good once bottled. Casks are an investment best left to the distillers themselves.

RELATED TOPIC
See also
COLLECTING WHISKEY
page 130

3-SECOND NIP
Increasing rarity and burgeoning demand have seen certain bottles of whiskey become a cult alternative investment.

3-MINUTE DISTILLATION
Whiskey's far easier to store than wine and it lasts much longer too: A sealed bottle is perfectly happy at room temperature, kept upright so the strength of alcohol doesn't corrode cork stoppers, stored out of direct sunlight, and hidden away from thirsty guests. Like any investment, there are risks. Drop it or open it and a bottle is clearly worthless. In certain countries/states, selling can be a challenge due to licensing laws.

3-SECOND BIOGRAPHIES
GIUSEPPE BEGNONI
1951–
Italian whiskey enthusiast said to own the largest collection in the world

CLAIVE VIDIZ
1934–
Brazilian whisky enthusiast whose collection of 3,384 bottles is now on permanent display at the Scotch Whisky Experience, Edinburgh

EXPERT
Andy Simpson

Certain whiskey bottles and decanters can be a very wise investment. In 2010, a Lalique Cire Perdue decanter of The Macallan 64-year-old whisky was sold at auction for $460,000.

APPRECIATION

development How the aroma and taste of a whiskey changes; the final stage in considering its flavor profile.

flavor wheel A graphic device to display whiskey's aromatic and taste characteristics first devised by Pentland Scotch Whisky Research (now The Scotch Whisky Research Institute within Heriot Watt University, Edinburgh) in 1978. Cardinal aromatic groups form the wheel's "hub" (typically: cereal, floral, fruity, peaty, woody, winey, etc.), each being broken down at the next level (thus "fruity" might break down into "fresh fruit," "cooked fruit," "dried fruit," "canned fruit") and the outer "rim" of the wheel into more specific aromas (so "dried fruit" might be divided into "raisins," "sultanas," "figs," "dates," "mince pies," "Christmas cake," "marmalade"). The descriptors serve as a guide to help you come up with your own.

Glencairn glass Invented by Raymond Davidson, founder of Glencairn Crystal in East Kilbride, in about 1980, but not launched until 2001, this is designed to present both aroma and taste to best advantage.

highball The original highball was simply Scotch and soda, served with ice in a 6 or 8 ounce glass, but the term is sometimes extended to any long iced drink with a spirit base topped with any carbonated beverage. Recently the drink was reinvented in Japan as a "Suntory Highball," with much success.

legs "Legs" or "tears" form when you swirl the liquid and observe the droplets as they trickle down the inside of the glass. Thick, slow-running legs indicate a viscous texture; skinny, fast-running legs, the opposite.

Manhattan Recognized as "one of the six basic cocktails," the Manhattan is simply equal parts of Italian (sweet) vermouth and either bourbon or rye, over ice, with a dash of Angostura bitters added to each glass.

Mint Julep Classically made with good Kentucky bourbon, the Mint Julep is a long iced drink, typically served in a metal tumbler. Gently bruise a dozen mint leaves with a tablespoon of sugar syrup and two or three dashes of Angostura bitters. Add 2 ounces of whiskey and stir. Chill the julep glasses, fill with ice, add the julep mix, stir gently, and garnish with mint leaves. This is *the* drink of the Kentucky Derby.

mouthfeel effects An assessment of the texture of the liquid in the mouth: warming, cooling, coating, astringent, fizzy (spritzich).

nosefeel effects An assessment of the physical effect the alcohol has when you sniff it: hot (alcoholic, peppery, prickly) or cool (mentholated, eucalyptic, drying).

nosing The term used to describe "smelling." Unlike "wine tasters," "whiskey tasters" are referred to as "noses" and a tasting session as a "nosing and tasting."

olfactory receptors Smells are detected by the olfactory epithelium, a small pad of mucous-covered cell tissue located behind and slightly above our noses. Our sense of smell is infinitely more acute than that of taste; while we are equipped with around 9,000 taste buds, we have between 50 and 100 million olfactory receptors, capable of identifying aromas diluted to miniscule amounts.

organoleptic Assessing the smell, taste, and texture (touch) of a substance with our senses.

primary tastes The four primary tastes are sweet, sour (acidic), salty, and bitter. When we think we are "tasting" more than this, we are in fact being influenced by odors identified by our olfactory epithelium via our retro-nasal passage. Try holding your nose while tasting, and see how this limits what you can taste. A fifth primary taste, umami (loosely described as "savory") was identified by a Japanese chemist in 1909, but only accepted in the 1990s.

Rob Roy Named after the Highland freebooter made famous by Sir Walter Scott in his novel of the same name, the Rob Roy is simply a Manhattan made with Scotch. Experts advise that Peychaud bitters replace Angostura. A variation is the Bobbie Burns, to which a dash of Drambuie whisky liqueur is added.

Rusty Nail A cocktail combining around 75 percent Scotch and 25 percent Drambuie whisky liqueur, stirred over block ice.

Sazerac "A sharp, pungent, thoroughly dry cocktail" (David A. Embury). Stir with large ice cubes, 1 teaspoon sugar syrup, 3 dashes Peychaud bitters, 2.5 ounces straight rye whiskey. Rinse the chilled old-fashioned glass with absinthe. Garnish with a twist of lemon peel.

viscimetry Viscimation occurs when two liquids of different viscosity mix, creating eddies and whorls. You can observe this phenomenon, briefly, when you add water to whiskey. The capacity of a liquid to create such can be termed its viscimetric potential.

WHISKEY VERSATILITY

3-SECOND NIP
Whiskey is a sublime drink enjoyed on its own, but its versatility means that it can equally be explored in more creative ways.

3-MINUTE DISTILLATION
Whiskey concoctions vary globally. In Japan, whisky and soda make a refreshing highball. America's famous Kentucky Derby is toasted with the Mint Julep, made with mint, sugar, bourbon, and soda. Head north and the Manhattan's rich vibes end the day with its layering of whiskey (traditionally Canadian rye), vermouth, and bitters. Substitute with Scotch and you have a Rob Roy. In Ireland, Irish coffee perks up the morning, while the secret infusion of herbs, sugar, honey, spices, and whisky that is Drambuie combine perfectly with Scotch whisky to form the Rusty Nail.

While modern-day purists may suggest that drinking whiskey neat is the only way to go, that wouldn't do justice to the drink's historical roots. Two centuries back, rough and unaged whiskey would have been enhanced by being infused with herbs, fruits, or spices. By the nineteenth century whiskey punches and cocktails were being served— such as the Sazerac, created in New Orleans in the 1830s, originally made using French brandy but subsequently modified to use American rye whiskey and absinthe. When phylloxera devastated vines in Europe the worldwide shortage of brandy helped fuel interest in whiskey. Bartenders looked for alternatives to use in their creations and whiskey was a common sense go-to. By the twentieth century, maturing whiskey in barrel was the law or common practice in most countries, and that addition of oak softened the spirit, bringing forward more vanilla, toffee, or spicy flavors. With its incredible array of fruity, savory, spicy, sweet, oaky, and grassy notes, whiskey can play a part in everything from cocktails to cakes and savory dishes—an extremely versatile ingredient that chefs and whiskey professionals are increasingly exploring.

RELATED TOPIC
See also
WHISKEY & FOOD
page 150

EXPERT
Alwynne Gwilt

Famous whisk(e)y and bourbon cocktails include (top to bottom) the Sazerac, the Mint Julep, the Rob Roy, the Irish coffee, and the Rusty Nail.

SERVING WHISKEY

Whiskey is supremely versatile:

long or short; with or without ice or mixers (typically soda, ginger ale, lemonade, or green tea), as a base for a cocktail, to refresh or comfort, as an aperitif or a digestif ... To best appreciate its flavor there are two simple rules: Use a glass which presents the aroma to full advantage; and add a little water—this opens up the aroma and makes it easier to taste. The whiskey will be bottled at the strength the maker felt most appropriate—unless the bottle states that the whiskey is "cask strength" it will have been diluted to the strength indicated on the label. If you are adding water, ensure that it has no smell (chlorine or minerals, for example) or taste. The ideal water is from the area where the whiskey was made. Try adding a drop or two at a time until the right strength is achieved for you. Ice can do wonders on a hot day, but by adding it, you put the whiskey in lock-down, and stop many of the aromatic molecules from becoming volatile so you can smell them. Also, don't neglect how you store the precious liquid. A dark cupboard, away from direct sunlight, is best. Store your bottles upright, not horizontal. Since the aging process halts when the liquid is bottled, your whiskey keeps for a long time without major changes. But beware: Once you open the bottle, the liquid will begin to alter.

RELATED TOPICS
See also
NOSING & TASTING
page 142

WHISKEY & FOOD
page 150

EXPERT
Alwynne Gwilt

3-SECOND NIP
How you choose to enjoy your whiskey is up to you—pleasure is individual.

3-MINUTE DISTILLATION
The vessel in which the whiskey is served is also important. Popular tumblers feel more relaxed in the hand, but the wide rim means the whiskey's aroma will not seem as concentrated. In short: they look classy, but are for more casual drinking experiences. A more classic glass has a bulbous bowl and a rim that narrows to concentrate the aroma and thereby enhance the organoleptic experience.

Whether you like your whiskey straight or "on the rocks," the shape of the glass is key to enhancing the pleasures of the dram.

NOSING & TASTING

Professionals assess whiskey

quality organoleptically, that is by "sensory evaluation," using four of our five senses to evaluate flavor (sight, smell, touch, taste). First, we consider a whiskey's appearance—color, clarity, viscimetry, viscosity. The color hints at the cask(s) the whiskey was matured in—malts finished in bourbon casks tend to be tinged gold whereas sherry casks result in a darker-hued spirit. When the whiskey is swirled the "legs" that trickle down the glass provide a clue to "mouthfeel": Slow thick legs indicate good texture/viscosity. Viscimetric whorls shimmer momentarily when water is added—another indication of texture. Second, we nose the whiskey noting, initially, its physical effect or "nosefeel" (if any)—sharp, prickly, warming, cooling—then try to identify what we are smelling—perhaps honey, smoky peat, oaky vanilla, or salty coastal notes. Third, from a small sip we assess texture or "mouthfeel" (smooth, oily, astringent, mouth-filling, etc.) and taste (sweet, sour/acidic, salty, bitter/dry). Fourth, we add a small amount of water to open up the aroma and make it more comfortable to assess the taste. Finally, we set the sample aside ten minutes or so, then nose it again to see how it might have changed (this is called "development").

3-SECOND NIP
Enjoy whiskey as you choose; full appreciation follows an established procedure to explore smell, taste, and texture.

3-MINUTE DISTILLATION
Because of the importance of the aroma in appreciating whiskey, it is essential to use a glass that displays this to best advantage, i.e. one with a bowl (to swirl the liquid) and a rim that narrows (to concentrate the aroma and direct it up the nose). Adding water helps (how much is personal preference), but definitely no ice, since this reduces the aroma significantly. If adding water makes the whiskey hazy, it has not been chill-filtered.

RELATED TOPICS
See also
WHISKEY VERSATILITY
page 138

SERVING WHISKEY
page 140

DESCRIBING FLAVOR
page 146

3-SECOND BIOGRAPHIES
RAYMOND DAVIDSON
1947–
Founder of Glencairn Crystal and inventor of the "Glencairn Glass" for nosing and tasting whiskey

RICHARD PATERSON
1949–
Scottish Master Blender and an expert—and charismatic—"noser"

EXPERT
Charles MacLean

All but one of our five senses are key to a proper appreciation of whiskey.

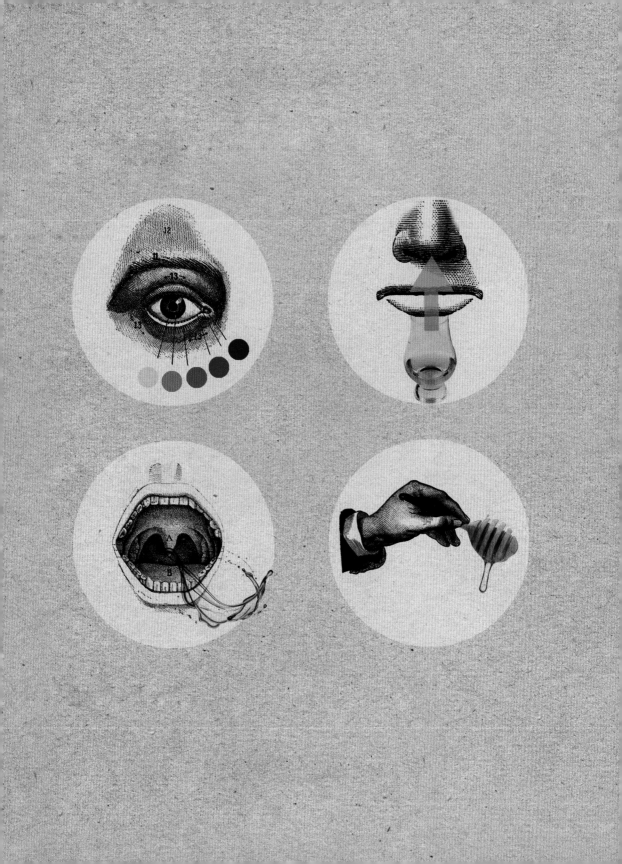

1960
Born at Greenock, Renfrewshire, Scotland into a family who had worked as brewers and distillers during the nineteenth century—as well as being enthusiastic whisky consumers

1965–78
Schooled at Greenock Academy, where he discovers a love of science, especially biochemistry and biology

1978–83
Studies for degree at Glasgow University, majoring in Cell Biology and Biochemistry BSc (Hons), and becomes serious about quality alcohol—mainly real ale and wine

1983–86
Accepted by Heriot Watt University's Department of Brewing and Biological Sciences to write a doctoral thesis relating to the science of fermentation. Much influenced by grain scientist Professor Sir Geoff Palmer

1984
First taste of Glenmorangie and malt whisky, begins to study the technical aspects of production in parallel with his PhD work

1987
Marries Leslie Hoggan, the Principal's secretary at Heriot Watt

1988
Offered a job as a research scientist by the Distillers Company Ltd. Primarily involved in front end production— malting, mashing, fermenting. Develops a special interest in flavor and its provenance, inspired particularly by Dr. Jim Beveridge who specialized in flavor development during maturation

1990–93
Signs up to a training program for malt distillery managers, which includes spells in quality assurance and in grain distilling

1995
Joins Glenmorangie plc, as Distillery Manager

1998–2012
Moves to Glenmorangie's head office in Edinburgh as Head of Distilleries— in charge of all whisky production

2012
Appointed to the Board as Director of Distilling and Whisky Creation

BILL LUMSDEN

Bill Lumsden has been at the forefront of whisky innovation for the past 20 years, indeed he has been aptly described as "The Great Innovator."

Known in the trade as "Dr. Bill," the Director of Distilling and Whisky Creation at Glenmorangie has earned universal respect for his innovations in maturing Scotch, and particularly for his experimentation with finishing. As he puts it:

From early in my career, I knew that no matter how good the raw spirit, if it's not matured in good quality oak you simply cannot make good whisky.

After he moved to Glenmorangie at the start of 1995, he had the opportunity to supervise and control production of this famous malt whisky from Tain, and after three years as Manager here, he was given responsibility for the other two distilleries in the Group at that time (Ardbeg on Islay and Glen Moray, Elgin).

He viewed the distilleries not simply as whisky production sites but as full-scale laboratories, and set about developing a range of new products. At the outset, he had inherited the remnants of a wood-management program, investigating how the flavor of Glenmorangie was influenced by different cask types. It soon became apparent to him that total maturation in most of these casks masked the delicate character of the whisky.

Undeterred, he went on to explore the little known technique of "wood-finishing," where the spirit is matured in the traditional way, then transferred to casks which had previously contained other wines or spirits for the final months or years of its maturation in order to add another layer of flavor. Between 1995 and 2005, Dr. Bill introduced over 20 new expressions of Glenmorangie, finished in various ex-wine and spirit casks: port, sherry, Madeira, Malaga, Bordeaux, Sauternes, Cognac, etc. Many other distillers followed his example.

The acquisition of The Glenmorangie Company by luxury goods giant LVMH (Louis Vuitton Moët Hennessy) in 2005 provided Dr. Bill with even more opportunities for experimentation. The single malt *Glenmorangie Signet* uses a portion of high roast chocolate malt; *Glenmorangie Tùsail* uses the now rare Maris Otter barley variety; *Glenmorangie Ealanta* was wholly matured for 19 years in virgin American oak casks; *Ardbeg Uigeadail* is a combination of whiskies matured in ex-bourbon and ex-sherry casks.

Increasingly Dr. Bill combines his whisky creation with global travel as Glenmorangie's key brand ambassador. Now in his 50s he has many more years of innovation in him before he finally hangs up his lab coat.

Charles MacLean

DESCRIBING FLAVOR

3-SECOND NIP
Describing flavor is difficult and takes practice, but it focuses the mind, raises awareness, and stimulates appreciation.

3-MINUTE DISTILLATION
Flavor wheels identify several cardinal aromatic groups (Grainy, Grassy, Fruity, Woody etc.). The second tier breaks these down further, while a third tier serves to suggest descriptors which might arise in subjective assessment. By way of example, "Grainy" might be the initial identification but, with practice, the sensory evaluation becomes ever-more exact, moving to "Cereal: breakfast cereal, porridge, grits, bran, toast, digestive biscuits" or "Malt: malted milk, malt barn, dried hops, Marmite (yeast extract)."

It is often forgotten that "flavor" is a combination of smell, taste, and texture. Smell is the most important for quality assessment/appreciation: While we are equipped with around 9,000 tastebuds, we have between 50 and 100 million olfactory receptors and can identify odors in miniscule amounts—commonly in a few parts per million (one ppm is equivalent to 1cm in 10km), sometimes in parts per billion (one ppb = 1cm in 10,000km) and occasionally in parts per trillion (1ppt = 1cm in 10 million km, or 250 times the circumference of Earth). Such sensitivity means that "the human instrument" is more acute than any machine yet invented, which is why whiskey quality is still assessed by humans. But humans must communicate their findings, and it is famously difficult to describe smells. The language used can either be strictly objective/analytical (vocabulary-controlled, assessors-trained) or subjective/hedonic, that is, use whatever descriptors come to mind, however personal; figurative language is commonly used: "smells like . . . ," "reminds me of . . ." The first attempt to systematize the language of whiskey assessment was made by Pentlands Scotch Whisky Research in 1978 and displayed in the form of a "Flavour Wheel." A simplified version for consumers helps to unite mind, body, and spirit.

RELATED TOPICS
See also
WHISKEY VERSATILITY
page 138

SERVING WHISKEY
page 140

NOSING & TASTING
page 142

3-SECOND BIOGRAPHY
DR JIM SWAN
1941–
One of the authors of the Pentlands Wheel and now a leading adviser on the construction of new distilleries

EXPERT
Charles MacLean

The Pentlands Wheel was devised for use by the trade; a simplified flavor wheel showing the eight aroma groups is illustrated here.

AGE STATEMENTS

RELATED TOPICS
See also
SCOTCH & NON-SCOTCH
page 18

BOURBON
page 98

EXPERT
Gavin D. Smith

3-SECOND NIP
When a whiskey carries an age statement, the age in question must by law refer to the youngest component whiskey in the bottle.

3-MINUTE DISTILLATION
Increasing sales of both Scotch whisky and US bourbon in recent years have led to a situation where many distillers find themselves short of stocks of mature spirit. Accordingly, they have had to remove age statements from existing bottlings or create new NAS expressions, persuading consumers that these expressions are not inferior to those carrying age statements. Inevitably, some NAS whiskeys—which tend to include amounts of younger spirit in their composition—are of higher quality than others, and consumer opinion is divided on their virtues.

For much of the commercial existence of whiskey, age statements were never a consideration. Whiskey tended to be drunk raw and new or at a relatively young age. In the UK, the first stipulation of a minimum age at which Scotch whisky could be sold came in 1915, when the Liquor Control Board set the minimum age at two years as a measure to reduce drunkenness among munitions workers. It was believed that drinking new spirit led to greater inebriation than imbibing older whisky. The minimum age was increased to three years in 1916. Until well into the twentieth century, most bottled Scotch whisky was offered at between five and ten years of age, though Johnnie Walker put a 12-year-old age statement on its Black Label brand in 1906, and sales soared. Indeed, age has often been considered synonymous with quality by consumers, whereas the reality is rarely as simple as that. Many established distillers now offer a range of aged expressions stretching from 12 to 18 or 25 years, though some, such as Ardbeg, Glenmorangie, and Bruichladdich, have made policy decisions not to place age statements on most of their releases. These are known as non-age-statement (or NAS) bottlings.

Age statements refer to the length of time that the whiskey has been matured in the barrel. The oldest whisky is a Mortlach 75-year-old, bottled by Gordon & MacPhail.

WHISKEY & FOOD

Serving whiskey with food may

not be traditional but it has become popular for additional enjoyment. A successful match is based on sensory evaluation, always starting from the whiskey's aromatic profile, identifying the best ingredients to complement or contrast its flavors. For instance, you may choose to balance sour or bitter notes with a honeyed sauce. The same applies to texture: You can oppose a smooth mouthfeel to crunchy vegetables or enhance a rich velvety whiskey with a creamy sauce. Taken individually, a whiskey and a dish have their own richness and personality. When (well) matched, they create additional character, introducing new flavors. The type of cask in which the whiskey is matured is a key element to consider. Whiskeys matured in bourbon casks tend to be light and fresh with a caramel sweetness and vanilla notes from the new oak. They complement fish, shellfish, salads, poultry, fruit, and custard desserts. Whiskeys matured in sherry casks (especially if they are made from European oak) are more tannic and pair better with red meat (beef, venison), rich sauces, raisins and dates, mature cheeses, and chocolate. Peated whiskeys combine perfectly with shellfish—oysters in particular—blue cheeses and citrus fruit, but they should never be paired with smoked food as the two types of smoke will clash.

RELATED TOPICS
See also
MATURING
page 62

NOSING & TASTING
page 142

3-SECOND NIP
Pairing whiskey and food is all about finding harmony and balance by achieving a good match of flavors and textures.

3-MINUTE DISTILLATION
Cooking with whiskey follows the same principles as pairing. Brief marinating, deglazing, and spraying whiskey on hot food are effective techniques but *flambé* should be avoided—the alcohol evaporates and the flavors too. One word of warning: Avoid garlic as its pungent flavor overwhelms even the most stalwart whiskey; garlic kills vampires but it also slays whiskey.

3-SECOND BIOGRAPHY
OLIVIER ROELLINGER
1955–
French chef and an extraordinary spice blender with great expertise in culinary sensory evaluation

EXPERT
Martine Nouet

When pairing whiskeys with food, check which type of cask your dram has been matured in, so you can match your whiskey with its complementary flavors.

WHISKEY FESTIVALS

3-SECOND NIP

An excellent way to get acquainted with various whiskeys, their producers, and like-minded enthusiasts is to attend a whiskey festival; they are held annually, worldwide.

3-MINUTE DISTILLATION

With increasing numbers of festivals, free-spirited whiskey-lovers can gather in their thousands to share their passion. The quirkiest and most relaxed festival around is Maltstock, modeled after Woodstock. It is held annually in early September at a scout camp in the woods in Nijmegen in the Netherlands. Enthusiasts from around the world bring their own bottles and enjoy drams, music, food, and talks for a whole weekend.

The first whiskey festival ever may be the Kentucky Bourbon Festival, which began in 1992 as an evening in Bardstown, KY and is now an annual staple: a whiskey week with multitudes of events for young and old. In 1998 John and Amy Hansell launched WhiskyFest in NYC, a one-day event now held in Chicago, San Francisco, and Washington, D.C. The British launched a similar event in 2000, Whisky Live London, franchised to other countries including Australia, France, Ireland, South Africa, Japan, and Taiwan. The year 2000 also witnessed the birth of the Spirit of Speyside Festival, a five-day event in the eponymous Scottish region, with over 250 venues. The Isle of Islay has held Feis Ile since 2001: During eight days each Islay distillery hosts an open day. Across Europe there is a plethora of festivals, such as the two-day Whisky Fair in Limburg, Germany, loved by collectors, while the Netherlands hosts two three-day events, The International Whisky Festival in The Hague and the Whisky Festival Northern Netherlands (WFNN) in Groningen. Apart from masterclasses in nosing and tasting, many festivals also offer a feast for other senses, selling books, clothes, food, and merchandise to celebrate the noble spirit.

3-SECOND BIOGRAPHY
JOHN HANSELL
1960–

American writer/publisher, founder of Whiskyfest in 1998, an offspring of his magazine *Malt Advocate* (in later years renamed *Whisky Advocate*), and considered to be the inventor of the modern-day whiskey festival

EXPERT
Hans Offringa

Whiskey festivals have become increasingly popular and numerous in recent decades and there are now many to choose from, hosted in countries all around the world.

NOTES ON CONTRIBUTORS

EDITOR

Charles MacLean has been described by *The Times* as "Scotland's leading whisky expert." He has been researching and writing about whisk(e)y for 35 years, and has published 15 books on the subject. He was founding editor of *Whisky Magazine* (1997), is a regular contributor to publications, and has written historical and promotional materials for all the leading Scotch whisky companies. He was elected a Keeper of the Quaich in 1992, and elevated to Master of the Quaich in 2009.

FOREWORD

Ian Buxton is an author, commentator, and consultant with some 30 years' experience in the drinks industry. He writes for a number of trade and consumer magazines and his books—including the bestselling *101 Whiskies to Try Before You Die*—have been translated into eight different languages.

AUTHORS

Davin de Kergommeaux is the author of the award-winning book *Canadian Whisky: The Portable Expert*. He stopped making bricks, playing music, and tending gardens after six university years studying whisky grains. He founded the Canadian Whisky Awards, and publishes notes about Canadian whisky on canadianwhisky.org. His social media alias is @Davindek.

Alwynne Gwilt is the Whisky Specialist with William Grant & Sons, UK. She was one of the first female whisky bloggers with her site *Miss Whisky*, founded in 2011 and has been named one of the Top 10 Women in Whisky. She has contributed to numerous magazines and newspapers globally, and runs whiskey tastings and trainings around the UK.

Angus MacRaild is a freelance whisky writer based in Leith, Edinburgh. He has a background in whisky auctioneering and is a leading authority on old and rare whiskies. He hosts regular specialist tastings of these whiskies around the UK and Europe and writes for various online and print publications.

Marcin Miller is a Master of the Quaich, Rectifier of the Gin Guild and Liveryman of the Worshipful Company of Distillers. Launch publisher of *Whisky Magazine* and contributor to numerous books and magazines, he co-founded Number One Drinks Company in 2006. His latest project is Japan's first purpose-built gin distillery.

Arthur Motley is a director at Royal Mile Whiskies and Drinkmonger and has been a whisky buyer all his working life, beginning as cask buyer for the Scotch Malt Whisky Society in the year 2000. He is proud to be a Keeper of the Quaich and a Champagne Academician.

Martine Nouet is a French-born author and journalist who writes about food and spirits exclusively. Martine has pioneered a new trend in the world of whiskey: the sensory idea of pairing whiskeys with a suitable food counterpart. She was elevated to a Master of the Quaich in April 2012.

Fionnán O'Connor is a drinks critic and historian living in Dublin, where he serves on the committee of the Irish Whiskey Society. He has written articles for publications across the industry and recently represented the Irish whiskey category before the European Union. His *A Glass Apart: Irish Single Pot Still Whiskey* was published in 2015.

Hans Offringa is a bilingual author and media expert, who has specialized in writing and presenting about whisk(e)y since 1990 and has published more than 25 books and hundreds of articles around the globe. The European Contributing Editor of *Whisky Magazine*, he has been awarded with the titles of Honorary Scotsman, Kentucky Colonel, and Keeper of the Quaich.

Andy Simpson is a Keeper of the Quaich and has been an avid whisky collector from the age of 16. He is now a professional whisky valuer, broker, and consultant to the Scotch whisky industry. Co-founding Director of Rare Whisky 101, Andy regularly provides comment and analysis for the media and has been featured in the *Financial Times*, the *Wall Street Journal*, *New York Times*, *Forbes*, *GQ*, *The Guardian*, the specialist drinks press, and many other publications. Andy lives in rural Perthshire with his wife Kayte and young son Jacob.

Gavin D. Smith is a Scottish-based professional freelance writer. He is the author and co-author of some 20 books devoted to whisky. As a journalist he contributes on a regular basis to a wide range of drinks publications and is Commissioning Editor, Scotland for *Whisky Magazine*. His work also regularly appears online at *www.scotchwhisky.com* and *www.cuttingspirit.com*. Additionally he undertakes writing commissions for leading drinks companies and hosts whisky events.

RESOURCES

BOOKS

*A Glass Apart: Irish Single
Pot Still Whiskey*
Fionnán O'Connor
(Images Publishing, 2015)

*À Table: Whisky from
Glass to Plate*
Martine Nouet
(Ailsa Press, 2016)

*American Whiskey, Bourbon
& Rye: A Guide to the
Nation's Favorite Spirit*
Clay Risen
(Sterling Epicure, 2013)

*Canadian Whisky:
The Portable Expert*
Davin de Kergommeaux
(McClelland & Stewart;
1st edn, 2012)

*Goodness Nose: The
Passionate Revelations of a
Scotch Whisky Master Blender*
Richard Paterson &
Gavin D. Smith
(Neil Wilson Publishing, 2010)

*Irish Whiskey: A History
of Distilling in Ireland*
E. B. McGuire
(Gill and Macmillan, 1973)

*Japanese Whisky, Scotch
Blend: The Japanese Whisky
King and His Scotch Wife*
Olive Checkland
(Scottish Cultural Press, 2001)

Malt Whisky Yearbook 2017
Ingvar Ronde
(MagDig Media Ltd; 12th
edn, 2016)

*Peat Smoke and Spirit:
A Portrait of Islay and
its Whiskies*
Andrew Jefford
(Headline, 2005)

*The Best Collection of
Malt Scotch Whisky*
Valentino Zagatti
(Formagrafica, 1999)

*Last Call: The Rise and
Fall of Prohibition*
Daniel Okrent
(Scribner; 1st edn, 2011)

The World Atlas of Whisky
Dave Broom
(Mitchell Beazley;
2nd edn, 2014)

*Scotch Whisky:
A Liquid History*
Charles MacLean
(Cassell Illustrated, 2005)

Whisky
Aeneas MacDonald
(Canongate US, 2007
[originally published 1930])

Whiskey Opus
Gavin D. Smith &
Dominic Roskrow
(DK, 2012)

*Whiskey Women: The Untold
Story of How Women Saved
Bourbon, Scotch, and Irish
Whiskey*
Fred Minnick
(Potomac Books, 2013)

FESTIVALS

Kentucky Bourbon Festival
A week-long festival held in Bardstown every fall. It attracts over 50,000 people from a dozen different countries to participate in more than 30 events.

Kentucky Bourbon Trail
An official trail that embraces a selection of distilleries and brand centers, offering an impressive visitor experience.

Maltstock
Weekend festival held in early September in Nijmegen, in the Netherlands. Highlights are the whiskey quiz, the detox walk, and the BBQ party and campfire session.

The Whisky Fair, Limburg
Europe's largest and most important whiskey festival.

The Whisky Show, London
The UK's biggest and most important show for novices and professionals alike.

RETAILERS

Gordon & MacPhail
Founded in 1895 as a grocery store, this Elgin-based retailer has grown into so much more. They have bought and bottled their own casks for over a century, recently bottling the oldest aged-stated whisky in history: a Mortlach 75 Year Old. In 1998 they purchased Benromach distillery.

Royal Mile Whiskies
Founded in 1991 and bought by Keir Sword in 1995, this Edinburgh retailer has a thriving web business, and has had a store in London since 2002. Regarded for their range, friendly service, and down-to-earth approach.

The Whisky Exchange
Sukhinder Singh went from being a passionate collector to one of the most powerful figures in alcohol retail in little over a decade. Beginning online, their Covent Garden, London, store showcases the huge array of fine whiskeys now available.

WEBSITES

Canadian Whisky
canadianwhisky.org
Author Davin de Kergommeaux's blog about Canadian whiskies.

Japanese Whisky
nonjatta.com
A comprehensive and independent guide to the Japanese whisky scene.

Rare Whisky 101
rarewhisky101.com
Whisky consultancy that provides the industry standard indices on Scotch as an investment.

Scotch Whisky
scotchwhisky.com
Home to *Whiskypedia*, a comprehensive online guide to the world of Scotch whisky.

Whisky Advocate Blog
whiskyadvocate.com/blog
The online *Whisky Advocate* magazine blog.

INDEX

ACKNOWLEDGMENTS

PICTURE CREDITS

The publisher would like to thank the following individuals and organizations for their kind permission to reproduce the images in this book. Every effort has been made to acknowledge the pictures; however, we apologize if there are any unintentional omissions. All images are Shutterstock or ClipArt.com unless otherwise stated.

Adelphi Distillery: 119C. Alamy: 916 collection: 33TR; Chris James: 131TL; Doug Houghton SCO: 75T; DV Oenology: 131BSR; Gary Doak: 133SL; Granger Historical Picture Archive: 31C; Heritage Image Partnership Ltd: 117TL; John Peter Photography: 87C; Lordprice Collection: 35B, 35C, 35CR, 35T; Scottish Viewpoint: 77BL; travelib: 31BR; Universal Images Group North America LLC / DeAgostini: 77C, 126, 133FR, 131BSL. Andy Simpson: 131FL; 131FR; 131TR. Asahi Beer: 106. Ben Nuttall (via Flickr): 83TC. Beam Suntory: 38; 99BL. Bladnoch Distillery: 83BL. British Library: 33TC; 79C. Bridgeman Images: 33C. Brown-Forman Corporation: GlenDronach images appear courtesy of The BenRiach Distillery Company Limited. GLENDRONACH is a registered trademark of The BenRiach Distillery Limited: 79T, 79B, 79FL, 79FR, 149; Jack Daniel's images appear courtesy of Jack Daniel's Properties, Inc. JACK DANIEL'S is a registered trademark of Jack Daniel's Properties, Inc.: 19FL, 101BL; Woodford Reserve images appear courtesy of Brown-Forman Corporation. Woodford Reserve is a registered trademark of Brown-Forman Corporation: 99TR. Charles MacLean (*Whisky Magazine*): 9. Diageo: 19SR; 75BR; 81BC. Dominic Lockyer (via Flickr): 97TL. Getty Images: De Agostini Picture Library: 57CFR; Jeff J. Mitchell: 133TCL, 133TCR; Mike Clarke: 133TC; Science & Society Picture Library: 31TR, 35C, 117TCL; Tim Graham: 57BFR, 91CR. Glenmorangie: 75C. Glenora Distillers: 103SL. Heaven Hill: 99TL. Hood River Distillers: 103FR. Ian MacLeod Distillers: 77T.

iStock: 77CFR; 81BC; 81CL; 89C. John Distilleries: 109BR. Lark Distillery: 109BL; 109R. Library of Congress, Washington DC: 37C; 41TC; 41BL; 41BR; 43C (warehouse background); 45BC; 45C; 77C; 101TC; 101C; 103C; 105CR. Library and Archives Canada: 43B. National Library of Ireland: 63B. Nigab Pressbuilder (via Flickr): 97TC. Number One Drinks Company: 45CL; 45CT; 45CR; 105TL; 105BL–R; 105C. The Keepers of the Quaich: 121C, 121B. The Scotch Malt Whisky Society: 125T; 125CR. Svensk Whisky AB: 111C. The Whisky Exchange: 129C (window display). Topfoto: Mike Wilkinson: 64. Valerie Hinojosa (via Flickr): 57BC. Wellcome Library, London: 21TC; 21C; 22; 22; 25C; 25T; 25B; 103TL. Whyte & Mackay: 75BL. Wikimedia Commons: Rvalette: 22SR; Brian Stansberry: 101TL. William Grant & Sons: 84. William Murphy (via Flickr): 97CR. Stephen Yeargin (via Flickr): 101BC.

We also wish to thank the following for their kind permission to depict their brands in this book:

Amrut Distilleries: 109TL. Ardbeg Distillery: 89L. Asahi Beer: Nikka Whisky: 19FR. Beam Suntory: Ardmore: 79B; Auchentoshan: 83BR; Bowmore: 89R, 131FR; Canadian Club: 103SR; Glen Garioch: 79B; Hiram Walker & Sons: 43C; Jim Beam: 99BR; Laphroaig: 89C; Maker's Mark: 99C. Bladnoch Distillery: 83TR. Burn Stewart Distillers: Deanston: 81TL, 81BL. Chivas Brothers: Green Spot: 97TR; Redbreast: 19C; The Glenlivet: 31BC, 31BR, 87T & BL, 117TR. Diageo: Bell's: 117TTL; Clynelish: 75BR; Crown Royal: 19SL, 103FL; George Dickel: 101TC; Johnnie Walker: 19SR, 31TR, 117TL; Oban: 77BC; Talisker: 91TR, 91BR. Gordon & MacPhail: 131BCL, 133BL. Signatory Vintage Scotch Whisky Co. Ltd.: Edradour: 81BR. Springbank Whisky: 77C; 77BR; 131TL; 133TCL. Teeling Whiskey: 97TL. Whyte & Mackay: Jura: 91C (x2). William Grant & Sons: Balvenie: 87BC; Glenfiddich: 87BR, 133TCR; Tullamore Dew: 97TC.